Hoosiers and Hippies

Hoosiers and Hippies

by

Jerry Beisler

For Betty Larsen my friend for life and love in the next lifetime.

Jerry Beisler

Regent Press
Berkeley, CA

Paperback:
ISBN 13: 978-1-58790-497-4
ISBN 10: 1-58790-497-7

E-Book
ISBN 13: 978-1-58790-498-1
ISBN 10: 1-58790-498-5

Library of Congress Catalog Number: *forthcoming*

Printed in the U.S.A.
REGENT PRESS
Berkeley, California
www.regentpress.net

Acknowledgments

Special thanks to MeanderlyArt for contributing graphic art, formatting and editing to every page. It was an inspiration.

Sharon Zarkin: you put the ROCK in rock 'n' roll.

My eternal gratitude to cover artist Andrew Annenberg, who also contributed the front and back covers of *The Bandit of Kabul, The Berkeley Years,* and *Hawaiian Life and the Pink Dolphins*; illustrations for many of my magazine articles and newspaper features; and the cover art for several musical singles I co-wrote or produced.

*Why does evil exist? It thickens
the plot.*

—Rama Krishna

*There must be more to life than
having everything.*

—Maurice Sendak

*Whitey's on the moon
Ain't no money here
But whitey's on the moon*

—Gil Scott Heron

*Work my hammer for the factory
Foreman always wanna fight
And then swallow up a TV dinner
Swing my hammer strong at night*

—Captain Beef Hart,
"Hard Work Drivin' Man"

*No human's knowledge
shall go beyond their
experiences.*

—John Locke, "Essay
Concerning
Human Understanding" (1690)

*In the Halls of Justice
the only Justice is in the Halls.*

—Lenny Bruce

*Vietnam was the first war fought
without censorship. Without
censorship things can get terribly
confused in the
public mind.*

—General William Westmoreland

*They say marijuana is
addictive…I know it's not because
I've smoked it every day for 55
years.*

—Louis Armstrong

*Man considering is the most
formidable of beasts of prey and,
indeed, the only one that preys
statistically on
its own species.*

—William James, *Memories and
Studies*

*There's nothing half so sweet in
life
as love's young dream.*

—Thomas Moore

*To live outside the law
you must be honest.*

—Bob Dylan

Just because it is... does not mean it should be.

—Lady Sarah Ashley

Let's begin with the ending. I run out of a burning building, two guns pointed to the heavens blasting, dive in to the back seat of a car driven by a true, unique beauty. The tires squeal and we are outta there. Escaping the decade of the sixties was something real close to that and here's how it started.

Chapter One

I don't run around with no mob.
Got myself a little job.
I'm gonna buy me a little car,
Drive my girl in the park.
Don't bother me, leave me alone.
Anyway I'm almost grown.

—Chuck Berry

There were three things to aspire to for males in the small, weekend-tourist beach town I grew up in: varsity athlete, a position in student government, and lifeguard. The town hosted, as the sun roasted, an estimated three thousand tourists during the big summer holidays and hot spells.

One mile of Lake Michigan's sandy shore was lifeguard domain. It was required before going on duty that the guards run a mile and then swim a quarter mile. Everyone enjoyed that start to the day's work, as physical fitness was a unanimous lifestyle choice. A large faux-Mediterranean seaside style building, constructed as a public works project, centered the beach and housed changing rooms, a burger joint, and a lounge rental stand. We guards had our own locker room facing the water and adorned by a first aid poster. On the walls were framed photos chronicling decades past of guard crews mixed with faded newspaper clippings of heroic, life-saving rescues.

Behind the locker room, to the side of the toilet, was a room originally built to house kayaks. Kayaks

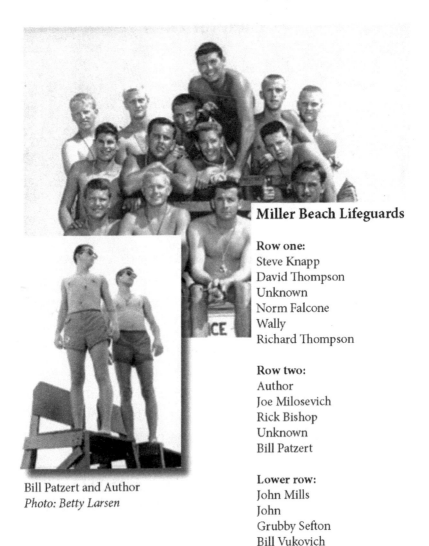

Miller Beach Lifeguards

Row one:
Steve Knapp
David Thompson
Unknown
Norm Falcone
Wally
Richard Thompson

Row two:
Author
Joe Milosevich
Rick Bishop
Unknown
Bill Patzert

Lower row:
John Mills
John
Grubby Sefton
Bill Vukovich

Bill Patzert and Author
Photo: Betty Larsen

proved too unstable because of Lake Michigan's notorious, deadly reputation for incredibly quick changes of weather and water conditions. Undertows, squalls and lightning storms were always a potential 20 minutes away. The old kayak closet locked from the inside and had a sign on the door proclaiming "Movie Stars Only." It was sparsely furnished with a foam

12

rubber pad, ratty blanket and pillow. On the walls were magazine stories of B-movie star Ronald Reagan. All of the articles related that Reagan had been a lifeguard in his hometown from age fourteen until twenty-two. Reagan was credited with seventy-seven saves by various writers. There was a photo of Reagan wearing a wool bathing suit with an emblem on the front as well as a photo of the plaque honoring the 77-save heroism.

Cardboard was stapled to the inside of the door. Printed on it years before was a handwritten question about the people who inhabited the town of Dixon, Illinois, where Reagan was a lifeguard. The writer imagined a conversation that might have taken place in that town:

"Madge, the kids want to go swimming today."

"But, dear, haven't 11... 23... 45... 90 children almost drowned!?"

"I believe it's only 77, Madge... must be safe enough! And Ron Reagan's the lifeguard!"

The message was signed "Charles Darwin."

Another perk was the use of the roof of the beach house for a traditional monthly "Guards Party." The Parks Department allowed one keg, officially.

Chapter Two

I always imagined that Paradise will be a library.

—Jorge Luis Borges

How "it," life, politics and payoffs work came to me the second summer as a lifeguard.

My brother Randy, after one month's practice and being almost unaware of the competition, had won the Indiana State Championship in shotput during the spring. He joined me on the Guards that summer, at what in no way was a job to me.

The mile-long beach with a snack shop on each end hosted thousands of tourists on busy weekends. It was idyllic until the assistant head guard, Graham "Grubby and Grumpy" Sefton, ascended to head guard. All guards called him Grubby on the whole, although Grumpy came to the forefront.

Fifty years of guard tradition, such as no longer allowing "a private lunch with a new friend from Chicago in the guards' quarters," ended. When that order went ignored like other petty new rules, Grubby kicked the door open during an afternoon's delight.

Also he set up a kickback operation with the tow truck driver by alerting the police when some far-corner illegal parking was "in violation." This meant he spent time wandering the thousand-car lot, cutting our break and lunch times. I came to know it because at the beachside snack shack, the tow truck driver, in a whisper, suggested the quasi-scam to me! Two and two said Grumpy, with a beach towel draped over his guard outfit, wasn't looking for the Holy Grail.

In a fit of what looked to me like jealous rage, Grubby fired my brother with two weeks left in the season. I vigorously protested and was fired as well.

To be a lifeguard was a very prestigious job. You had to prove your physical fitness as well as being sponsored. Our neighbor and the father of one of our best friends was a major politician, and our sponsor.

"Not *my* boys," he said.

Grubby pushed: "Insubordination, tardiness and 'distraction by the females.'"

"Didn't Jerry have two saves this year... both in the newspaper and *one* on national radio?" my sponsor argued.

There was a settlement. So as not to create a fissure in Grumpy's authority, for the last two weeks we were both fired. We were both given double our two weeks' pay and could pick it up the next day. We agreed and signed.

Grubby was accepted into the Police Academy.

My brother and I were packed for the airport when we picked up our checks, cashed them and got on the express bus for our flight to Miami. I had an idea that we start our vacation in the Castaways, right on the strip. The appeal was that the Castaways had a bar with glass behind it where you could see the swimming pool's underwater frolic. I had heard about it being a first and thus I assumed it would attract like-minded "out of the box" people.

I was right. We got a Nash Rambler at the airport, put aside enough money to get home, and began non-stop fun, all starting at the bar, where you watched talented synchronized swimmers mixed with bathing suit tops and bottoms pulled up and down.

It always seemed to set a frisky mood.

Chapter Three

*Education is the ability to listen to almost anything
without losing your temper.*

—Robert Frost

My next-door
neighbors in the Indiana
University athletic dorm
were both seniors, Earl
Faison and Roy Pratt. Faison
and Pratt were the starting
defensive ends on the IU
football team.

Room 101-A was,
as the number notes, much
smaller than any other dorm
room, so my roommate and
I slept head-to-toe and ate
food nose-to-nose. I was
admitted three days before

Earl Faison at IU

school started. My roommate was also a late admission,
because he had spent a year after high school traveling
to the world's great events, seeing the Royal Ascot horse
races, the 24 Hours of Le Mans speedwagons, famous
opera singer Maria Callas performing in Italy, and the
World Series, to cite a few. I saw the photo album of his
glorious time during the week we shared the room.

He became uncomfortable when Earl and Roy
and I, with a rotating fourth hand, played Whist in our

room. There were a number of lovers of the card game around but it had to be played "when immediately possible" because of the myriad obligations we all had.

I wasn't shocked when my roommate moved out so soon. Nor was I surprised when he queried rhetorically as he packed, "You *really* get along with those guys? It's been a lesson of possibilities for me."

"Cool guys," I said, adding, "Roy went to Froebel... a high school rival. He grew up about 10 miles from me."

At the door, he stunned me by saying, "You know, you should learn how to talk. I could only understand about half of what you say. Another student told me you talk Calumet Region Rat Language."

The language from the streets of Gary put a lot of "ain't it so" at the end of sentences, as well as a positive reply always including some form of, "that'll make the news." A comparison to Cockney would be too extreme but nonetheless, it had a number of idioms unique to a city that enjoyed a great integration of diversity: Greektown, the Black entertainment district, Miller Beach, and of course the Steel Mills would produce "call bullshit on that."

Roy Pratt and Earl Faison both spoke the King's English and never swore. The two men were dedicated to their studies and constantly trying to be better ball players. I followed their lead.

Also I had 101-A to myself. Besides Whist, for fun I started a "coin pull from the winning pot" poker game, weekend bed rental, and a host of other entrepreneurial opportunities, with Roy and Earl as my silent Vice Presidents. The unused shelves were

18

soon filled with athletic department t-shirts, sweats, hats, baseball gloves and balls, cigars, and a football, individually priced.

Freshman football coach "Goon" Brown noticed the price tags when he entered my room, saying, "Campus Police had you in a report on a big beer party on this floor."

"Yeah," I replied. "When Earl signed that 1st round draft choice for a pro football contract, he threw a party for his teammates to celebrate. He asked me to go out and explain what was being celebrated to Campus Police."

"That right?" Goon Brown growled.

"Earl paid to have the whole place cleaned up, and told the officers, and they came back and it was spic and span... end of story, Coach."

"What about this stuff?" Coach Brown questioned, pointing at the shelves. "That Earl's and Roy's?"

"No way, Coach," I said. "Earl signed for six figures and Roy is student teaching and working, since football's over. That is *consigned* by juniors and sophomores with no money."

"That so," he questioned with more than a hint of anger.

"Don't worry, Coach. Next semester I have a roommate, so there won't be any place for this *extra money* scene. Anyway, we're all going home for Christmas break and they'll be needing it for presents."

Next semester arrived and I wasn't assigned a roommate. It confirmed one of the tenets I'd learned in my Intro to Business class... Location, location, location.

Chapter Four

If you reject the food, ignore the customs, fear the religion,
and avoid the people, you might as well stay home.

—James Michener

My eyesight deteriorated, which led to the Student Government pursuit. Glasses were a kick down towards the dork end of teenageville. Popular media culture reinforced the idea of dweebdom in every visual image and verbal message. I had already experienced going from a kid star pitcher in baseball to sport-ending arm injury at 18. In basketball, situational playing time and no further

Student Government: Sall Pierce,
author and Karen Wojohn

interest from any of the cheerleaders was the curse of "Goggles," "Specs," and "Mr. McGoo."

The first thing my freshman college coach Bill Ring did, to my great benefit, was send me for contact lenses. My swish at the dish came back. I earned a "practice" role of emulating the opponent's best shooter.

A broken ankle the third week of practice my sophomore year dashed my hopes of making it as a "walk on" basketball player at Indiana University. It began a basketball journey that no other has ever taken. As the ankle healed and the semester break approached, I began trying to grab a scholarship to one of the smaller schools that had recruited me out of high school. Three replied with tentative, "tryout" offers that included a dorm room, cafeteria pass and Greyhound bus ticket. I am a Saluki in Carbondale, Illinois in January 1963.

Coaches have a way of separating the "cowards" and "lazys" from the team. Coaches use the same method to "punish" players who anger them. It's called the "Loose Ball Drill." The coach skids the basketball between two or three players. The players are expected to aggressively dive onto the hardwood floor and fight for possession of the ball. Many times heads bang, elbows and knees scrape, noses break or shoulders separate. I was a deadeye, long-distance shooter. I did not enjoy going around the basket to rebound the ball with all the angry frustration and elbows flying, from men a foot taller and 40 pounds heavier. I enjoyed, less so, the Loose Ball Drill. My reward was another bus ticket.

I found myself in Bowling Green, Kentucky. The college was nicknamed "The Hill Toppers." This was due to an idea of the school's founding philanthropist that the students should walk a mile uphill to begin their day. My stay might have been longer if there had not been a zero degree cold spell. Combine the reluctance to go outside with the long, necessary walk to basketball practice and the result is you will find that dorm room and cafeteria privileges vanish.

Food and a bed were available at a small college in Tennessee. I am on a bus to a small school somewhere, with a religious denomination in its name. I'm optimistically hoping that since it's in the South it should be warmer.

While standing in a Quonset-hut gym with bleachers that held a thousand spectators, my newest coach said, "It's the coldest spell we've had around these parts in 14 years. It's bound to get better... right?" I wholeheartedly agreed. The first time we disagreed was when my new coach shouted, "Loose Ball Drill!" Add to this the night before in the "athletic" dorm. One of the jocks that I had a two-day, beer-fueled kinship with confided he had sex with animals as part of farm life out there in the country's heartland. After that tale, true or teasing, my mind went into a hazy, confused state and remained there until I heard again, "Loose Ball Drill!"

The following day I heard a woman behind a desk, wringing her hands and sweating profusely, say, "You have two more days here and you were never officially enrolled." I was relieved. Just before those final forty-eight hours were up, I received a fortunate phone call. Jubilation! My next stop on the odyssey was going to be Mexico City, Mexico... sun, *cerveza* and *señoritas* as a member of the North American All Stars.

An IRS agent who was the father of a high school friend obtained the position on the team for me. My friend's father had been on a task force that included FBI and Treasury Department personnel, which had investigated and helped convict corrupt politicians and judges in Gary, Indiana. He had then been transferred to Washington, D.C. He became aware of an immediate need for basketball players to participate in a "Goodwill Mission"; his new IRS tasks had something to do with reviewing the tax implications and necessary bureaucratic paperwork. He called his son and his son, God bless him, tracked me down, hungry and desperate in Tennessee. A room in the Zona Rosa, where the wealthiest Mexicans lived, became my home. *¿Hola jefe, dónde es la comida dinero?* (Hey Boss, are you paying for dinner?)

In 1963, the United States State Department implemented a *goodwill program* known as "People to People." Great musicians who could barely sell a ticket at home were paid well and sent abroad on tours. Similarly, a track team representing America in this outreach endeavor was sent to the USSR. The "North American All Stars" basketball team was the second in a goodwill tour of a foreign country.

One thing left out of the itinerary of the All Stars that should not have been: Mexico = *turistas*, or "the trots" to use the Anglo slang. When the "trots" hit the newly assembled squad, a mutiny occurred and a quartet of players demanded and received tickets home. The desperate staff and coach needed warm bodies quick! I was one of the replacements. The All Stars

23

were scheduled to play college and local club teams in a dozen major Mexican cities including Vera Cruz, Monterey, Guadalajara, Pueblo and culminating with a game against the Mexican National team on the major holiday of Cinco de Mayo in Mexico City's big Arena. But, first, inoculations for typhoid and yellow fever that makes one very, very sick.

Coach Williams was an intelligent, sophisticated, Spanish-speaking African-American from a small college near Washington, DC. He did a masterful job at the "welcoming banquet" in each city we played and a masterful job of culturally leading the team through various crises that would pop up.

Protests of "*Yanqui* go home" overall were small and in only three or four places. The opposing players were small as well so Coach Williams could play everyone; rest sprained ankles, poked eyes and dislocated fingers; and win every game.

Everything changed in the game in Pueblo because student radicals had called a strike in "our" name and succeeded in closing down much of the city as well as all of the University. The welcoming banquet was canceled, of course, after our bus was pelted with eggs and tomatoes. "Can't do no harm, eggs and tomatoes, men... This was a carefully planned *'allowed'* demonstration," Coach Williams counseled. He added, "That's how they do things down here."

The basketball court was surrounded by scores of police with their backs to the game, which started testy and rough but quickly became another routine victory because of our far superior players. As the final buzzer sounded however, we were pelted by small coins and serenaded with boos and derogatory whistles. Still in our uniforms, we were all forced to sit on the floor of the bus. Blankets had been hastily taped to the windows during the game in anticipation of a gauntlet of thrown objects that would not be tomatoes or eggs while exiting Pueblo. *Crash, crack* and the sound of pounding placards on the vehicle's carriage was our "adios" while Coach Williams stepped around us down the bus aisle passing out tepid Coca Cola's and Snickers bars for a "job well done under difficult conditions."

It was a big, all-day bullfight fiesta on May 5, 1963 in Mexico City. Cinco de Mayo's sports dessert that holiday evening would be the Mexico National team's total destruction of the no-longer billed "North American All Stars," but the newly renamed "United States All Stars." We had not seen a player over 6'6" on our tour. The Mexico National team had won the Bronze Medal a year before in the Pan American

Games. All three front line players were right at seven feet. The core of the team had been together since playing in the previous Olympic Games. Succinctly, it was a 120 plus to low 70s drubbing the All Stars received. For me, it was more like standing in the middle of a track meet. My line, as I recall, was 0 in shots made, 0-1 in free throws made and 3 in personal fouls. The following day the team was treated to a party and buffet lunch and presented with five hundred dollars and a plane ticket to the States.

I would remain in Mexico, however, because the gods of basketball smiled and bequeathed to me a scholarship to Mexico City College. "Any of you guys want a scholarship down here?" Coach Williams offered. "Mexico City College is starting a team down here in the fall basketball season but the scholarship starts NOW... with summer school." I accepted, with gratitude, Coach Williams' offer and enrolled for my two hots and better than a cot; plus, there was no organized practice until September.

Mexico City College was primarily a school for rich kids who could not pass the foreign language requirements at the U.S. universities they attended. Family legacies, power and wealth could buy their way through business, law or medical school but you can either speak, read and write in the foreign tongue or not. Mexico City College offered an immersion program where one year of learning to speak and read Spanish counted as completing the two-year standard foreign language requirement at all affiliated U.S. Schools.

The school was built on top of a mountain, a

*Author in front of Mexico City
College scholarship dorm
Photo: Larry Lindeen*

winding six miles up from Mexico City, on the Toluca Highway. All the buildings were nice, Colonial Style with earth tone tile roofs. There was a cafeteria that served American-style breakfast and lunch and there was a twenty-unit "scholarship" dormitory where I would live.

Most of the students commuted to campus by bus up from apartments and rooms in the Zona Rosa district. Some drove Corvettes and Thunderbirds. A small village abutted the campus and supplemented specifically the scholarship students' needs and desires. Since the cafeteria was not open at night, we scholarship students had to avail ourselves of the village taco wagon or bus it down the mountain for dinner.

Over the years, the "needs and desires" of the student were equal to the taco wagon's entrepreneurial skills in many, many areas.

"I defended Trotsky's assassin. I saved him from the death penalty," my professor of Mexican history stated. And it was true. The distinguished, trilingual, retired legal scholar, as a young practicing attorney, had defended Trotsky's killer and gotten him a thirty-year sentence. He brought history to life with his masterful use of language, measured dramatics and "to-be-continued" cliffhangers.

My two other classes, written and conversational Spanish language courses, were so useful in everyday life that I worked on them enthusiastically. Also, I was trying to find a way to make some money. Traditional collegiate methods such as selling fake IDs were a no-go in Mexico. The students at Mexico City College did not need a fake anything to get "anything." In fact, the students at MC City, as they called Mexico City College, invented the "Shoot the Mad-Dog Rainbow." They mixed "mucho" tequila with a green chili, a yellow mango and slices of red pepper, and pasted it all together with white refried beans. The concoction was eaten to induce vomiting, which did come quickly. Thus the mad-dog rainbow.

I was "living down" the 500 dollars now converted to pesos. I had no choice but to carry it on me at all times.

Chapter Five

I needed the shelter of someone's arms
and there you were
I needed someone to understand my ups and downs
and there you were
With sweet love and devotion
Deeply touching my emotion

—Marvin Gaye, "How Sweet It Is (To Be Loved By You)

I had never been happier than when a girl showed genuine interest in me, open and offering, like Doreen did. Puppy love, first love, long-distance love, eagerly awaited love letters and self-initiated treachery-betrayal love, and the nuances and subtleties surrounding these tiny bits called "Love" had been my previous experience.

In the culture of the day, most kids were tossed into a mixing of the genders with a little knowledge gleaned from movies, pop songs and "forbidden" racy books. The mating ritual was usually a drunken bacchanal. Doreen had never been drunk. Everything I learned, I learned quick. Doreen was on summer break from Trinity College in Toronto. She was spending school vacation in Mexico City, where her parents were "up there" in the Canadian Embassy. She had been given a horse as a welcoming gift. When she was 16, Doreen won a literary competition and became Summerset Maugham's pen pal for a year. He was so charmed by her writing skills he invited her and her parents to his villa on the French Riviera.

She liked me. Then she loved me. A wave of
civility and consciousness comfortably overcame me.
I was in love. It was a constant logistical nightmare
for us to get together. We had my dorm room, which
meant a dangerous late night Mexico City trip home
for us. Doreen, only 20, lived with her parents, and
the last Tolusa Rocket bus down the mountain that was
safe left before dark. Those difficulties often made
for a love affair of difficult desperation. We never
had a bad moment. Our minds were always working
together towards "next time."

We were an island separate from the mass
media, mindless manipulation of our peers at home.
The cliques, the social pressures and haves and have-
nots. True have-nots lived less than a half mile away
in mud-floor adobe huts, supplying us with dinner
from the taco wagon when Doreen could come up
with an excuse to stay all night.

Doreen's gift horse was kept at a picture perfect
Rancho that also stabled horses ridden in the Mexican
Charro, or Horse Ballet. The Charro was performed
by beautiful, highly trained horses in a show created
centuries ago in Spain. My mount was handsome and
stout and we headed out on a pleasure ride on a trail
that ringed the expansive Ranchero's lands. Doreen
was arena trained and schooled in equine manners. I
had been riding since I was a toddler and considered
a horseback ride to consist of a warm-up walk, then
a trot, a canter and a dead run as soon as the terrain

presented the opportunity.

At one point, Doreen and I flew by two women riding sidesaddle who unexpectedly appeared out of the foliage. The riders we flew past were startled, and then angry. After our ride, Doreen went from giddy to ghostly as she grasped what our icy reception was likely about as we dismounted at the stable. The incident led to a "command appearance" for the first time with her parents the next day.

"You're too big to be a jockey so you must be a c–o–w–boy," Doreen's father spelled it slowly and deliberately.

"We were just riding the horses and having some fun and we came on them, but it wasn't ever close," I replied, before adding a genuine and contrite, "I apologize if we scared anyone."

"So, you're Doreen's dirty little secret, eh?" said her mother.

There was a double-sharp knock on my dorm room door that proclaimed an importance or authority. It was "Torres, from the Canadian Embassy," as he introduced himself. Torres wore a summer suit and his hair was waxed into a dramatic style. "Doreen was in an automobile accident," he stated, standing proper and direct.

"What?" I stammered.

Torres answered, "I am to drive you to her if you wish."

"Let's go! *Vamaños*!"

"You'll need a warm coat. It's *muy frio* where we are going."

To a villa in the mountains of central Mexico, out of the capital's smoggy heat. Before we left, Torres said he had "no information about the accident, so don't ask."

Doreen's family had taken an annual summer vacation, and were afforded the top personnel at the embassy. Ciudad Victoria was our destination and it was an arduous, silent, and anxious journey. Torres, for all his pomp and circumstance, was actually only a driver for the Canadian embassy. He was quick to tell me that I spoke "gutter Spanish" when I tried to engage and gain a little language knowledge. Also, I realized soon enough that I should not talk to him or distract him in *any way* because of his arrogant, reckless approach to the dangerous and narrow Mexican highways.

Doreen was wearing a neck brace when I saw her. Her leg was heavily bandaged. "I'm all right... really, really lucky, and just banged around," she insisted immediately.

"Great!" I gushed happily. I approached her as if she would be as delicate as a soap bubble. Doreen's parents had taken the worst of the head-on collision. Her father was in serious condition and all the focus was on getting him to a hospital with state-of-the-art services.

I stayed in a small hotel in a room next to Torres' room. It was foggy and wet that morning. Doreen and I were allotted one hour before Torres was to drive me back to college. The frightening prospect of danger at every turn hovered over the time.

Doreen had a plan for us: I would finish the quarter in Mexico City and then move to Toronto, where we would become engaged to marry. We would attend "a school like Trinity, or Trinity itself." I said, "yes" to everything and anything. It was all hurried and too sad to take anything any way but seriously. Most of all, I wanted to keep Doreen.

It was time to go. "Take pictures of us, even though I only have these borrowed clothes," she asked Torres. He did. "I'll send the plan, the tickets, some money, everything from Toronto. This photo too!" Doreen exclaimed, through the "death trap car" window. We kissed goodbye and proclaimed our love.

Two weeks later, I got the photo and an initialed drawing that said, "sorry" around a drooping, sad-faced flower.

Chapter Six

It is better to have a permanent income
than be fascinating.

—Oscar Wilde

From the May 5th, Cinco de Mayo Day
basketball game to the day after Memorial Day at the
end of the month, I moved toward getting a summer
job at Inland Steel. The mills always hired college
students and began their first day of work the day
after the holiday until the day after Labor Day in early
September.

I used the return trip plane ticket originally
from Houston the state department had supplied, back
to Texas in a combination of train, bus and hitchhiking
toward the smokestacks, with a stop for a day or two
en route with a young lass I'd met on the way.

My brother received a full scholarship to play
football at Indiana University and would be joining
me there in the fall. Nonetheless, like for many other
hometown athletes, the steel mills were necessary
financially. Also mill work was a dollar more an hour
than being a lifeguard.

We were fortunate to be placed in Field Forces.
Since the mills employed thirty-three thousand
people, there was always a stack of framing lumber
or piles of heavy used bolts or propane empties that
needed to be hauled and replaced. The work took us
all over the factory and I quickly learned there were

instrument readers in air-conditioned rooms, hot filthy, dangerous work around molten steel, and scores of women in offices that needed bundles of paper or cardboard moved out. Railroad cars were loaded and unloaded. Trucks and ships as well. All of which needed secondary work.

The dirtiest place with putrid fumes from the process was called the Black Plate. I hated the one-a-week delivery and retrieval of propane tanks. Joe Jackson signed the tanks in and out. I got to know him by talking music. He was back in the mills after having been in a singing group called The Falcons. Unfortunately their hit record, "So Fine," which spawned the solo career of Wilson Pickett, came after Jackson left.

Joe Jackson talked music with me because I mentioned that I was a regular at the F and J Lounge when Buddy Guy played, or enthusiastically described sets I'd seen by Muddy Waters and Howlin' Wolf at Pepper's on Chicago's Southside. He began to greet me with, "Hey, music lover," when I came to replace the empty propane tanks.

Jackson had a slew of kids; he'd throw a name out concerning an upcoming birthday or recital, like Tito or Jermain. Jackson frequently lamented he had signed a bad contract with The Falcons, and so was "back in the Black Hole" until he got a family band together. "It won't be the blues, for sure," Jackson said. "No money in the blues... check out that junk car Buddy Guy drives."

Chapter Seven

I'm a city boy. When I hunt it's for a parking place,
when I fish it's for compliments.

—Jon Carroll

My brother's shepherd for an Indiana
University football scholarship entré was the Miller
Beach Biz Wiz. He had a pool hall, bowling alley and
insurance agency.

"I got a good idea for you we're gonna act on.
The Chicago White Sox offered me a shot at a tryout
with anyone I pick. That's you!"

"I haven't played since my senior year in high
school... but thanks for a great offer!" I said sincerely.

Biz Wiz said, "Here's how we're gonna do it.
You're gonna pitch in the Industrial League to get
ready."

My pitching days had ended on the mound
against Edison High when my arm went limp. I played
second base when I was a senior.

Biz Wiz was not deterred, saying, "You lost the
speedball but had the Uncle Charlie. You had both
the sweeping curveball and the 12 to six sinker. I'm
selling a one- or two-inning Reliever that can throw
up, down and sideways."

He caught my greater attention when he said,
"And starting after Labor Day I'm gonna pay you
more than you're getting as a lifeguard. You start
by throwing and working it back up for two weeks

and then I'll get you in for an inning a game two or three times to get ready for the tryout. Lifeguard-plus is your pay until that day, as long as I see you practicing."

Could this be how miracles work? It went like that general plan, including throwing my hook pitches in the Industrial League. Steel mills, car part factories and refineries had a long, tough baseball tradition of paid umpires and free beer swilling. A hitter tripled off my pitch and his beer was delivered to third base.

My high school/college friend and number one wingman Jim Armalavage is driving me to Comisky Park. His dad was a surgeon who laid a new Buick on him. I told him, "If I just get a Minor League contract

in Florida for the winter, this whole thing will be worth it!"

I put on a White Sox uniform and my own cleats and watched a couple hitters finish up and a pitching prospect throw fireballs. I went out and threw my best and fielded a few soft grounders and a bunt.

Jim Armalavage was all smiles as I headed for the tunnel. A man walked briskly up to meet me with hand out for a shake, and depositing what I assumed was a daughter in his wake. "Charlie Finley and I'm gonna buy the White Sox and they told me you're from Gary, Indiana, and *I'm* from Gary... *You* are gonna be the first player I sign!"

Winter in Florida beckons!

Only one thing came from it all. Finley would buy a team, but not the White Sox. I got a hearty handshake, a "We'll call you," and a Sox hat. My wingman got Charlie's daughter for a two-year relationship, which unfortunately had an element of I-don't-trust-you-around-certain-of-your-friends-and-you-know-who.

Chapter Eight

You can't always get what you want
But if you try sometimes
You get what you need

—The Rolling Stones

Mike Bloomfield, Elvin Bishop, Barry Goldberg, and two or three other older Beatnik-type guys were in a corner at Silvero's. We Gary, Indiana blues lovers were in another. After a night or two, the two crowds couldn't help but intertwine; it was a small toilet used in many ways.

Howlin' Wolf protected all of us from the stage when some animated young men stormed the venue, shouting, "No whites in our neighborhood, looking for prostitutes and trying to turn the neighborhood girls into whores!"

Silvero's held about 350, and had a lot of active security as it was. They came but it was the Wolf from the stage that ended it, when that gravel voice said through the microphone, "These boys here for the music, nothin' more, understand that?!" After giving a moment to see the crowd's reaction, he added, "And if I see you do harm to anyone I'm gonna come down there and crush your head like a cantaloupe."

The mistaken young men, from my vantage point, were very clean and well-dressed in a manner that suggested some sort of religious affiliation. They left quietly, and Howlin' Wolf used the incident in his introduction to "Smokestack Lightning."

At the other blues club I went to regularly, Pepper's Lounge, Muddy Waters headlined often. Muddy saw us often enough that he once gave me a mouth-to-ear-warning. Little Walter had a set coming up, but before he performed with Muddy he moved around accepting drinks and cigarettes. He interacted with us as he floated by, throwing out, "I'll be doin' 'My Babe' soon."

"I love that song!" I said loudly over the intermission din.

"*You* know 'My Babe'?" he chuckled, moving on.

I passed the stage as the show ended and Little Walter said to me, "Hey *My Babe*, come out back, smoke a cigarette after I hit the men's room."

Muddy Waters leaned over slightly and said to me, "Don't go anywhere with Little Walter... you get yourself killed... uh huh."

That was a quick turnaround from the musical euphoria. Little Walter had been brilliant on a half a dozen tunes that night, but under the glare of the post-show lights and breakdown racket, Muddy Waters' face was as a sage, prophet or oracle. That catapulted me into a "pay attention" journey to the car.

Chapter Nine

Peace in international affairs is a period of
lying and cheating between two periods of war. "

—Ambrose Bierce

In 1964 a television ad showed a lovely young girl counting the petals on a flower, and when she got to ten, an atomic bomb explosion filled the scene. It was an ad for Lyndon Johnson, the "peace" candidate, that implied his opponent, if elected, would go to war and possibly blow up the world. I cast my vote Johnson. The following summer, I was offered an especially high-paying job for my third summer of the steel mill work at United States Steel. It was 80 hours a week, with time and a half pay from 40-60 and then double time for any hours thereafter. The mill needed the 44-inch armor factory to re-open quick, thus the big bucks.

I took it and went 20 feet into a 60-foot deep pit. The 40 feet below had been used as a dump for broken everything – it was all hardened and mashed, and gallons of old oil accumulating since the 44" closed at the end of the Korean War.

There were two black veterans of that war and a white Purdue University student in the pit with me. We all wore hip waders because at any time, 500 gallons of oil would break loose. We four worked one side of a huge crane bucket and away it went.

It was horrible. Steel shoes, hard hat, gloves

and the rubber waders in an already hot facility was tough work. Lionel and Ray were the two mill vets, who called us "Purdue" and "IU". We were fortunate to have them, as safety was our concern number one. All four stuck it out and by early September the pit was clean.

One day, as the crane bucket was being hoisted and we had a short break, Ray said, "Got a war comin'... They don't open the 44 for *no* other reason, back to WWII."

"First I heard about it," said Purdue.

"Well," Lionel added, "44 makes armor and nothin' else."

"Where's it gonna be?" I asked.

Ray continued, turning two hands palms up. "They don't teach you college boys much in 1965, do they?" The bucket was coming back down. As we listened, he said with a finger point for emphasis, "Indo-China."

I looked it up later and saw the country was formerly called Indo-China, but now it was called Viet-Nam. Also it was about the size of Florida, and there was something going on militarily.

The next morning, I said to all three as we pulled, banged and shoveled, "Lionel and Ray were right. There's military stuff going on in Indo-China. But what you guys are wrong about is that the army would need any 44" armor 'cause the war ain't gonna last *that* long... The country's as big as Florida!"

Chapter Ten

*"Sort of" is a harmless thing to say, except after
"You're going to live," "It's a boy, or "I love you."*

—Demetri Martin

Lake Street in Miller Beach began as Highway 12 for automobile tourists and crossed the tracks of the South Shore that brought in others by rail from Chicago.

There was a Chinese restaurant, a sit-down pizza restaurant, an art gallery, and made-on-the-premises ice cream, mixed with a small town's professional medical, real estate and insurance offices, a pool hall/bar and bowling alley, and ending at Lake Michigan's shoreline asphalt parking lot and boat launch ramp. I parked to check potential water-skiing conditions. Slalom skiing was a new invention for the sport and was my current summer passion.

Marvin Berry and Pee Wee called my name. Marvin Berry was known locally as a vicious petty criminal who transferred to my high school for the final three months of my senior year. Berry in those short twelve weeks goaded many a classmate into a beating, bullied others, and showed up three days a week at school.

Short and stocky Pee Wee embraced the nickname by showing PEEE tattooed on his left-hand knuckles and WEEE on the other.

Here they are, talking over each other, saying,

"You're just the guy we been lookin' for." For what I can't imagine.

"Hey, Pee Wee," I said cordially, before asking, "I heard you moved back to Florida, Marvin."

"Some shit went down there and I'm back up here. But forget that horsecrap. We got easy money today. Three-way split."

"I ain't got time today 'cause I pick up my brother when he gets off work." It was a reminder of that brother who would help in a two-on-two later, if necessary.

Pee Wee wasn't going for two-on-one intimidation but actual assistance, in robbing four men that had gone toward No Man's Land down the beach. It was No Man's Land because in two miles, steel mill property began. Metal and concrete embankments and barbed wire ugliness. Plus, the locals believed the closer you went to the mills, the dirtier the water must be.

"They are queers... faggot wimps," Pee Wee said, adding, "We go down there about a mile and take their what they got like nothin'."

"They're rich fuck perverts from Illinois," Berry spat out. "We seen their new car and plates."

"They go to No Man's Land so no one can see 'em kissing," Pee Wee blurted. "We walk behind the dunes and see 'em. They fuckin' slow dance with each other."

"The only reason we need you is there's four of them. Me and Pee Wee been takin' on up to three... plus you being *right here* in the parking lot."

"I told you, I gotta pick up my brother... I'm

44

outta here," I said.

"Why you think they do that with each other?" Pee Wee asked, cupping his ear.

"I guess they love each other," I answered.

"What the fuck are you...?" Marvin Berry asked, taking an aggressive tone. I'd taken a psychology course and was well aware of displaced aggression.

Pee Wee puffed and barked, "You a fag all along and we didn't know!?"

"Are ya?" Marvin Berry snarled in my face, grabbing me by the collar with two hands.

I instantly headbutted him hard, breaking his nose, spattering blood profusely. I spun to take on Pee Wee and saw elbows, big buns bouncing and the soles of his shoes running across the parking lot. I was done but when, with his shirt up in his face to fight the bleeding, Marvin said, "I'll get you, mother–" I carefully calculated a kick to his testicles and left him rolling in pain.

Chapter Eleven

Of all the noises music is the least disagreeable.

—Samuel Johnson

One night on the southside of Chicago during a Jimmy Reed show's slow start I met Sam Lacy. Sam Lacy booked all the big names in Chicago Blues. The closest thing to a cross-over artist Lacy booked was Bo Diddley. Also, because of their great demand, Lacy booked bass and drums rhythm section Jerome Arnold and Sam Lacy as a unit.

Jimmy Reed was waiting for his amp, which had been picked up at a pawn shop and not handled well. It was part of a long list of problems Lacy had, booking headstrong talent like Muddy Waters and Howlin' Wolf. "Lady Bo" did all the business for Bo Diddley. One reason, Lacy said, Bo Diddley is on the radio is Lady Bo.

"Get me Bo and I'll put on a show, out where I live," I said.

Things moved quick. I rented an Elks Club that had a stage with money I collected from every male I knew. Since I had put on a couple of hellacious "dollar to get in" parties at IU, plus the old life guard, Mexico basketball tour, my brother on a football scholarship and some notorious deeds, I knew a lot of men. I promised two girls for every guy and to the females I offered free admission if they brought something to eat. Sam Lacy, delighted and happy to be tapping into the "white kids audience," agreed to take the money incrementally as I purchased a hundred pounds of cleaned big pink shrimp and the beer. More importantly was money put aside to pay the helpers for the beer and cleanup detail.

The place held 220 and it was full and right at the 2:1 gender ration. The ladies brought everything from their culinary specialties to a bag of potato chips. The band arrived and it wasn't Bo Diddley. The two beat-up station wagons delivered the Howlin' Wolf. His crew wanted to set up as fast as they could so they would be able to "get the hell outta here ASAP!"

That was a real benefit because by the time they brought out Howlin' Wolf's rocking chair I was fending off some irate beer-swilling "investors"... money back refund... no Bo Diddley—escalating complaints. I continued to dip into that big pile of pink shrimp and throw out compliments, as I sampled casseroles or mac and cheese with chopped peppers and onion.

I was comfortable because I knew what was soon to happen. And it did. The Wolf said, "We're happy to be here," and the band broke into "We Gonna Pitch a Wang Dang Doodle All Night Long" and everyone did.

Chapter Twelve

I believe that everyone my age is an adult
while I am merely in disguise.

—Margaret Atwood

Frank Brennan was on a tennis scholarship at IU out of the public courts, and not the country clubs that provided 90% of tennis players. He had New Jersey moxie blended with a desire to make the most of his sports scholarship, while being the most happy-go-lucky guy I'd ever known. We shared a 2-bedroom apartment our junior year, both shedding the athletic dorm as "once is enough."

I still had a buddy in another dorm complex and when I went to see him, lo and behold, Booker T. of Booker T. and the MG's. He'd had a huge hit with "Green Onions," and I gushed and blabbed when I met him. I loved the band and knew a little history of each player.

With humble gratitude, Booker T. invited me into his dorm room and walked me to the window. He pointed out with pride, "My new MG... I drove it to school from Memphis."

Indiana University was one of the top, if not the best, music schools in America. IU had its own classical music companies. The next time I visited my pal that lived next door to Booker T., I of course hoped to see Booker T. to find out if he or the band was going to be playing anywhere.

"Booker is gone," my buddy said, adding, "You know freshmen can't have cars and he had that MG *sports car*."

"We will never see him again," I predicted. "They got another hit breakin' on the radio *now*."

I was wrong. Booker T. left the car in Memphis, returned and attended IU for four years. The wonderful benefit I received was that a half dozen times, Booker T. played out in a small local club. When he did he had Lonnie Mack, the most innovative and experimental guitarist I had ever seen.

A late night TV talk show one-on-one interview format had Duke Ellington as a guest. The host asked him who the *greatest* was coming along. Without hesitation Duke Ellington said, "Booker T. Jones."

Chapter Thirteen

*Australia started as a prison colony, while
the USA is evolving into one.*

—Argus Hamilton

Marvin Berry returned to Florida to live a very short, unusual life. Newspapers in Florida document his criminal case and Berry's death in prison.

Berry hooked up with a felon named the Limper, who drove a 90-mile-an-hour cigarette boat carrying cocaine. Limper's court case reveals he got his handicap from being shot in the knee after trying to purloin the cocaine he was smuggling and getting caught. He had Berry convinced a couple he knew at the edge of town were a drop-off safe house and not cocaine pushers. The robbery and rape was on. The horrific act delayed their escape so, though remote, a neighbor called in "suspicious stuff going on" to the police. The news accounts sparked a compelling interest in Miller Beach as they unfolded.

The pizzazz of the eventual conviction of both men was Limpy powering a cigarette boat through the night at high speed. Cigarette boats had been developed to shoot across the 90 miles to Cuba to drop off operatives that sabotaged and damaged the primitive agriculture of the poor agrarian island. Bought from the government at maritime auction at the end of the covert operation, where American ingenuity quickly thought of ways to use the Cigarette to deliver things that need to be delivered *fast*.

The story was also jazzed up by Marvin Berry being only 21 years old and thus a storyline of a bad seed. Berry had been first convicted for going to apartment complexes' coin co-op washer/dryer areas and stealing all the quarters at 17.
Of course the savagery of the crime led to a sentence of thirty years, no parole for both men. Within nine months I did not have to worry about a shiv in the back in thirty years when Berry got out, because he was killed by another inmate.

Chapter Fourteen

Stay up all night, be dirty and wear filthy clothes. Tell the draft board
you're having acid flashbacks. It worked for The Byrds.

—David Crosby

An army recruiter whose three- or four-syllable name I never tried to say addressed me in an unexpectedly jocular manner. "You're the lucky son of a bitch that's my last recruit ever!"

"Yes, sir," I said, very much wanting to be accepted into the Army Reserve six-month active duty program.

"You don't have a draft notice, do you? That bullcrap is paperwork I ain't doin'... right?"

"No draft notice yet, sir," I answered. My last college class was over already; a few more days and my student deferment would be gone.

So Sergeant Four Syllable Name said, "Since my last day is Sunday, I'm sending you out with the sweetest deal there is."

"Yes, sir."

"Here's how it works," he stated, beginning to fill out my papers, "You listenin'?"

"Yes, sir."

"From here in Bloomington to Fort Knox is 110 miles. You can come home and bang your girlfriend on weekends. Why? 'Cause you're going to be a clerk in the motor pool. The clerk can always grab the last car on Friday night. Also they only keep ya for 4 1/2 months' active duty. That's all you need to learn, how to check cars in or out of a damn garage... Right?"

"Of course, sir," I affirmed immediately, with conviction.

"Well I told you it was the best situation as a recruit this army could ever dream up. Start signing here and here and I be picking up your medical records from the university. You don't got cooties or something?"

"Never had nothin' but the mumps and chicken pox type stuff when I was a kid, sir."

"Take this duffel bag," he said. "Put clothes and a toothbrush in it and meet me at the Greyhound Bus Saturday at 10 a.m... . Got it?"

"Got it, sir."

Saturday was three days away. I prepared to be a clerk in a motor pool, which sounded a whole lot better than the common verbal college theme that was all-pervasive, "Die in the rice paddies."

Saturday, Sgt. Four Syllable Name jerked to a stop and jumped out of his car waving papers, mad as hell. That's exactly what he said, "I'm mad as hell because some sawbones recommended you have surgery on a torn meniscus in your knee."

I remembered a knee sprain in a scrimmage three years before and the team doctor had said, "You have a little tear in your meniscus. If it *ever* gets worse I could go in and do a repair." I had never thought of it again.

"Gimme your papers," the Sergeant said with a

wave. Once I presented the papers, he scattered them on the roof of his car and then stamped them, hard.

"I had no idea, sir," I pleaded quietly.

He finished with, "I don't care what ideas you have, had or will ever have. I got to go to work on Monday and not be retired, that's the idea *I* have."

Chapter Fifteen

*It is far more impressive when others discover
your good qualities without your help.*

—Miss Manners

On Sunday in Indiana it was illegal to sell
liquor. This "Blue Law" meant that right across
the imaginary boundary line of Ohio you could
have shows with the very best emerging rock and
roll bands. The Fairgrounds venue was somewhat
equidistant from IU, Ball State and Butler. I saw
Them, with vocalist extraordinaire Van Morrison, and
got home feeling that the guitar work on "Mystic Eye"
was the best in the genre I ever heard. The Byrds had
their tight harmonies and avant-garde lead guitar on
some songs. That was fresh.

I'm close to front stage right, trying to slowly
work my way toward center stage with Sylvia Clark-
Hamilton, a wannabe rock photographer and avid
Cream fan who traveled there from Kentucky. I've
known her for thirty very promising minutes. I came
with two college buddies, and they suddenly appear
with an English-accent speaking guy they are having
an animated conversation with.

The English guy says, "So you put on the
Howlin' Wolf. What the bloody hell man... The boys
love him... Love that blues shit man," and he sticks
his hand out.

We shake and I say, "I grew up near Chicago

and I was lucky... got to see 'em all..." I throw out a half-dozen names of blues greats.

"And you put *on* the Wolf?" he says, giving a light push to my shoulder with a smile.

"Big night in my little home town... They are still talkin' about it!" I lightly boast.

"Two girls to every guy," one of my friends interjects.

Sylvia Clark-Hamilton took a firm grip on my arm. "You *got* to meet the boys backstage... Those are their heeeroes, man."

"Where should I meet you?" I asked the roadie.

He turned and pointed to a security guard at the stage's back left corner and said, "Right there, and give me ten minutes to tidy the fellas up."

"We'll be there," Sylvia Clark-Hamilton said.

Cream was doing 200 shows in 212 days and it showed. All three players not only looked exhausted, but they had dark circles under their eyes, pimples galore and were bone-skinny.

"So I heard you and the Howlin' Wolf did something, and that is so out there cool," Eric Clapton said to me. He put his foot up on a chair and took a half-eaten white bread and cheap steak sandwich out of his sock. Chewing with difficulty, Clapton mumbled something else unintelligible. The friendly roadie reappeared and offered it was time to go as he gave me another light, happy shove to the chest.

"Try and make the Fillmore show in San Francisco," Clapton said over his shoulder, still fighting the tough, cold sandwich. "*That* will be big!"

"I'll try, and it was tremendous to meet you!" I half shouted.

Sylvia asked, "Can I get a backstage pass *there*? The Fillmore?"

"*You* can count on that like the Bank of England," the friendly roadie said to Sylvia, turning his back to us and throwing in a hip shake as he left.

Chapter Sixteen

I've got all the money I need if I die by four o'clock.

—Henry Youngman

Beatles historians describe the band's meeting with Charlie Finley by recounting he appeared with a cashier's check for a hundred thousand dollars.

Charlie Finley, unable to buy the Chicago White Sox, had purchased the Kansas City Athletics, a team with few fans, no local history, and a long losing record. Finley became a rising showman-of-publicity character to promote the team. Though wealthy by Gary, Indiana standards, he was not old money with the ballpark named after the family owners.

I admired him because two decades before his success, he worked in the steel mills.

The Beatles were the biggest "sensation" in the world, in the middle of 30 gigs in 32 days across the USA. Beatles publicist and historian Derek Taylor records that the Beatles were in the back of their suite playing poker and smoking pot when their manager presented Finley's hundred-grand check. The Beatles quickly and unanimously refused to give up one of their two days off!

Finley went out to the bank and returned with a cashier's check for one hundred fifty thousand dollars. The Beatles said yes.

Finley wanted thirty-five minutes as soon as possible at the ballgame's finish. The Beatles said twenty minutes and Finley accepted, with the caveat that the Beatles play "I'm Going to Kansas City." They said they didn't know it... so no.

"No deal without 'I'm Going to Kansas City,'" Finley answered. The Beatles agreed to play it for one minute, twenty seconds. Finley shook hands with their manager.

What mattered to me was I was in a summer school apartment next door by happenstance to Charlie Finley Junior. I had met him previously, when my soon-to-be-former wingman began dating his sister after my White Sox tryout. One might think I would accompany him to see the Beatles. Unfortunately, Charlie Junior was a toddler when his dad became successful, and he immediately projected "I'm rich, you're not" in words and attitude: "I'm flying to Kansas City... first class, man."

"I'll drive; I'll meet you there," I countered.

Of course I don't know The Beatles are only going to play for 20 minutes. So I push my idea, "I'll drive and meet you there."

"Man, I'm gonna be in a limo and stuff like that. We are at different levels."

One level we were the same at was attending a month-long summer school "crash" course that students like myself had to dive into to pull the grades up to a "gentleman's C." Two hours of class in the morning and one hour each afternoon. I was taking an interesting course, Criminology. Learning things like how fingerprinting was invented, the period of time when they could tell a criminal by feeling their head, and childhood stories of infamous, top-ten-list bad folk.

After the hullaballoo that Charlie Senior had generated, and The Beatles had played to screaming girls for twenty minutes including singing, "I'm going to Kansas City" over and over for one minute and twenty seconds, Charlie Junior returned to his next-door apartment. I began to ask him a dozen questions but he interrupted in the middle of the first attempt of, "What did the Beatles kick it off with?"

Charlie Junior waved me off and said, "They have royalty in England, and I think when you're rich over here they think you're like royalty."

"And so..." I queried, hoping for a, "They were incredible, when they were playing–"

Instead Charlie Junior said, "So...! They treated *me* like royalty when I met them. They called me Prince Charles."

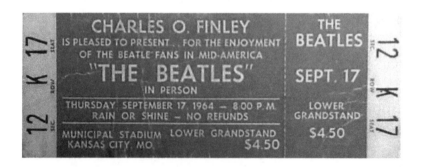

This and next page, the Beatles in Kansas City, 1964

Chapter Seventeen

This is the beginning of a new era in history.
And you can claim to have witnessed it.

—Johan Wolfgang von Goethe

Maxwell Street in Chicago hosted one of the world's Flea Markets. Its attraction to me, the 45 records of music, on the whole unavailable and half the price of the only inconvenient store. On card tables, in boxes, the music vendor had half a block.

There was Joe Jackson from the Black Plate Inland Steel.

"Hey Black Plate Boss," I said with a smile.

Jackson squinted his eyes, thought, and said, "That you, Music Lover?"

"Down here buying music," I replied.

"Who you got there?" Jackson asked.

"Ike and Tina Turner so far." I showed him the disk.

"They are good," Jackson was emphatic.

"First record I ever bought on Maxwell Street was 'Rock House' by Ray Charles."

"That's an instrumental," Jackson said. "Gotta groove." Haggling, music, and pedestrians bumped by. "You survived the steel mills too... Have a blessed day, Music Lover." Jackson smiled as he began to exit. Then he stopped, turned back, and handed me his card. "My kids have that band together and we're looking to play for money."

"I'll bet they are great. My kid brother's got a prom coming up at the Marguett Park Pavilion. I'll try that for you," I said.

"That's a beautiful building." Jackson said, then queried, "You finish college?"

"Yeah, I work in the Wrigley Building and just back to Gary for old friends and family."

"OK then," Jackson said. "*If* you put something together, it's gonna go like this... Me and the kids, instruments and amplifiers arrive to set up an hour before the prom starts, and you give me the money then... Right now or I don't unload and we leave."

The Jackson Five showed up and I paid Jackson. The prom started and four of the Jackson brothers laid down some dance-friendly sound and the kids were dancing. After a half hour or so Michael came out. He looked about 10 and I saw he knew how to sing in a child's high voice, dance, and *work* the mic.

"It's working out," I said to myself as I spotted my dancin' and prancin' young brother for a goodbye wave.

Joe Jackson was coming through then as I was leaving. He had a drumstick in his hand. He pointed to the stage and said, "He broke his stick... Look, he's playing with one hand and working the kick drum."

"I gotta go... got a date, but they are gonna be fantastic. I'll buy one of their records at Maxwell Street someday real soon."

Chapter Eighteen

Humankind cannot stand too much reality.

—T.S. Eliot

My Aunt Mary was a cantankerous woman whose daughter was a prim and proper major player in sorority society. I, having adored my cousin from childhood, was given the opportunity through her to date one of the IU cheerleaders, Jean Carol. The date lasted about 20 minutes because I could not resist a sideways slide down the sorority house's fabulous-looking (for a slide) two-story bannister.

I was with my aunt and her daughter, my brother, and a mixed gender group of friends at Indiana University's biggest college weekend: the Little 500. It was a bike race with a lot of tradition, great riders from other countries disguised as fraternity brothers, a big crowd, and lots of drinking. My aunt said the immortal words to one and all that would creep into a lot of jokes over the years: "The problem with Jerry and Randy is... their mother, my sister, did not beat them often enough or hard enough!"

My aunt had some valid observations beyond that, because for three summers of my life I spent a week or two on an Army Base hanging out, having a great time with my boy cousin known by one and all as Buddy. Buddy would become Cadet of Cadets at West Point.

Each year I visited him and his family. I would dutifully, at my parents' request, bring any athletic award I had received, such as Gary Indiana sixth grade basketball champs, or the Little League baseball all-star medal. Buddy was a champion swimmer, but at the time, other than the Olympics, swimming was an unknown sport. So his peers and he would greet me as a "star" athlete. Buddy would go to West Point and excel at that institution's unique standards, and also be a member of the NCAA winning medley relay swim sprint.

I held two views of war. One was from the movies, in which our good guys killed Native Americans and even our own fellow citizens in Civil War epics; those long-gone souls from many, many countries were killed at will while rarely suffering more than a wound or two.

Not the same in extended family versions at a half-dozen family gatherings. World War II didn't always come up at family parties, but when it did, Uncle Mike began drinking and would finish a quart bottle over the day. He cried, slobbered, and mumbled names and a word or two of description of each man he had recruited, in his role as a naval recruiter during WWII, who had been killed. Uncle Mike had played for a year in the National Football League. When the bottle was finished my other three uncles would help him to his car and dump him in the backseat.

Uncle Jakey had his testicles blown off in the famous Battle of the Bulge. I saw Uncle Jakey have to relive that fateful day painfully over and over as they tried to throw compliments his way for participating in the "Bulge."

Uncle John was a squat, powerful man who had survived the bitter, Pacific savagery of Iwo Jima and Guadacanel. When drunk, he would suddenly dart fast and grab one of the boys and give a "Dutch Rub" or hammer lock.

Uncle Paul had risen from Private to Colonel without having spent a minute in combat. He liked to brag how he came out of the Philippines in '46 with two suitcases so full of money, he had to sit on them to close them.

Now, there was his son Buddy in full uniform, taking the torch from those family war veterans, so no WWII talk. Instead, Vietnam "policy" and "strategy" and what so-and-so wrote about the war in the Chicago papers. Plus deserved praise for my brother for his college football success. The aunts were abuzz about impending marriages. Buddy and I had enjoyed a quick flyby lunch on his way to see his fiancée, a San Jose girl. I had a chance that day to tell him how very much I admired him for having not only the brains but to be tough enough to be a Ranger!

My Aunt Mary jumped in and recounted how even more worthless the Beisler brothers were compared to the officer and *gentleman* before us. She brayed, "The second summer Jerry stayed with his cousin, he got Buddy kicked out of the base Officers' swimming pool for pushing girls in."

Truly minor horseplay, but on a military base,

"Incidents such as this must be handled in a certain way," Uncle Paul explained to me, "So you're going to say you did it by yourself, understand?"

The truth was good enough: "I splashed two girls."

Immediately, in his uniform, my Uncle Paul drove 50 miles to the big city Greyhound depot and handed me a ticket to Gary, where horseplay at the beach with the Gary girls often ended with a water-soaked, thoroughly sand-covered towel across a boy's back; just a kind warning if you considered a Thermos bottle to the head an alternative show of a line being crossed.

Aunt Mary was onto my brother for say the 7th time in the last five family get-togethers. "We bring Randy down and within three days... three days!... he weighed fifty pounds more than Buddy, and a whole *head* taller... They are fighting each other!"

"We've heard it, we know what's coming," echoed from the familiar tale recipients.

Pointing, "*He* beat Buddy up!" For punishment, my brother had gotten a long, cold, silent, instant car trip all the way home, that he would mention and embellish to me more than once.

At our final ever family gathering, my Uncle John, not appreciative of my long hair and "likely attitudes that go with that Commie rats' nest," kept me ready to maybe have to knock him out. He was frothing at the mouth.

But I did get a quiet moment with Buddy before he left to wish him well and exchange addresses.

Besides "see you soon for one of Randy's football games," I told him to find a job like the one his dad held in the military, and come home with two suitcases so full of money you had to sit on them.

Instead he came home with the Congressional Medal of Honor.

Chapter Nineteen

Charlie you are my brother...
You're supposed to take care of me...
I could have been a contender. Now I'm a palooka.

—Ex-boxer Terry Malone as portrayed by
Marlon Brando in *On the Waterfront* (1954)

What began as a skirmish during 1960 between corporations with the creation of the American Football League became a corporate war by the mid-sixties. Signing high profile football players from the collegiate pool more and more came to symbolize the established National Football League's superior product. This mattered most in television, because popularity ratings meant advertising money to buy commercials during the surrounding hoopla and live game broadcasts.

The American Football league benefited from a far larger pool of available skill-set players than common knowledge said existed. Second-string quarterbacks became stars with playing time. Plus the AFL opened its rosters to players from the small traditionally Black conferences.

For television revenue, the competition to sign the Heisman Trophy winner and anointed first-round picks from the big name University All-Americans became fierce. Just before these prime prospects were eligible to sign their professional contracts, the NFL would hide the players in a tourist destination, which was usually warm as the draft of players was held in December. The men that escorted the players to these hiding places worked for the corporations that bought the advertising time on NFL games. These grunts in the corporate war were called baby sitters. The AFL countered with the same tactic.

This beauty contest draft did have a few slots for players unrecognized by reason of attending perennially losing, doormat schools—if they had true talent. My brother Randy was one of those. Indiana University was on total NCAA probation and won seven games in the three years Randy played there. Due to a severe shortage of actual players, Randy had to man both offensive and defensive tackle positions. Though he labored in obscurity in the trenches, suddenly a fairy godfather named Buck appeared promising tickets for a Chicago Bears game. Buck was a corporate Vice-President for one of the NFL's biggest advertisers of men's shaving products.

Buck said, "I'm here for you until draft day," and confirmed Randy was a Bears fan.

"Yea" Randy said.

"And you, you're his brother... probably a Bears man too?" Buck questioned.

"Nah," I answered casually, "the 49ers."

Buck's eyes flashed with genuine anger as he stammered, "To each his own I guess." Quickly, with a whisper and a wink, Buck spoke directly to Randy: "No napalm, no Agent Orange... no conscription once you're NFL. Yes sir," he concluded, "You got a shot at being a Chicago Bear!"

When he left, a hopeful Randy asked me, "Help

me get a car out of the deal, will you?"

Two weeks later, tickets for the 49ers–Bears game at Wrigley Field arrived in the mail with gas money. My brother and I attended with Buck and his teen-age son. My beloved 49ers were over matched. Gayle Sayers, the Bear's star running back, in a historic NFL game, scored six touchdowns.

Buck, somewhat tipsy from a pocket full of mini-bottle brandies, which he offered us throughout the game, gloated and teased me about the lopsided score. I took it good-naturedly, and he used that to get a bit demeaning. That was a mistake, as he earned my brother's never-ending enmity.

Randy heard from the American Football League as well, and it was bizarre too. The Boston Patriots offered a pre-dated contract with a $15,000 signing bonus and a one-year similar salary. It was presented to our family at dinner following another Indiana late-season loss, by the Patriots' rep.

When I said that figure was not close to what top players got, the Patriots representative said the owner of the team would talk directly to my father if he would go to a phone. In a few minutes a Mr. Sullivan was on the line, explaining to our father that big numbers were, "Hollywood-just-for-publicity figures... Sports page headlines... Nobody really got that kind of money!"

When my father told us he thought that was true, and Randy should sign the pre-dated offer, that was it for him and the Patriots. My brother and I agreed that I would be his agent and he would give me 10% if I got him $100,000 dollars. We both always heard agents for movie stars and singers got 10%.

I had one selling point at this moment: One sportswriter had cast a vote for my brother to be on the All-American college team. It made Randy an All-American honorable mention.

During the 60's most people's telephone numbers were listed. Mine was no exception and General Manger Carpenter of the Detroit Lions introduced himself by phone. "I understand you're helping your brother with the draft," he queried.

"I am."

"Would he be interested in the Lions?"

"Of course, Alex Karras is one of his local heroes," I answered. Karras, also from Gary, Indiana, was one of the Lions' biggest stars.

"What will it take financially to sign your brother?"

"Hundred thousand spread over three years; if he's no good you're not stuck with him," I answered quickly.

"I think we could work something like that out," Carpenter stated, his voice charged with certainty.

"Send me a telegram that says a hundred is good and we'll work it out by the draft," I stated honestly. When the telegram arrived no one was more astounded among my family and friends than me. Everything about Randy, from physical bearing to personal happiness, changed for the better.

Weeb Eubank, the coach of the New York Jets, called. After brief formalities, Coach, as he told me to address him, said, "I see Randy as a tight-end. I've seen film where he catches balls in the tackle eligible play; plus the speed. Randy is maybe the fastest lineman in the draft."

It was all I could want for my brother's career. "My brother catching passes from Joe Namath... Coach, sir," I gushed, "where do we sign up?"

"The Jets Chicago rep will call you and set up a place to go and get ready for the draft. Is that ok?" Coach asked.

"Absolutely," I confirmed.

Tom, the Jets baby sitter, phoned wondering if Randy and I wanted to hang out for a week or so. "NYC is cold... I was thinking of Miami."

I proposed, "How 'bout the Bahamas?"

Tom raved, "Jerry, you got good ideas. I'm gonna like hangin' out with you."

I was thrilled, crazed and excited when I told Randy what it meant to him. "New York City man... the bright lights... the commercial ads you could get maybe... and... hangin' with Broadway Joe!!" I foresaw seeing the musical *Hair* in the Theatre District...

Buck took us to the Bears practice. Two major things came from the experience. One of the Bears players was, like me, two years older than my brother, and I knew him well at Indiana University. "Go to any team but this one," he whispered. "This organization is beyond chickenshit-cheap. For example our punter

73

has to make league minimum and George Halas [the team's owner and coach] resents the minimum wage and makes every punter give money to Halas' charity of choice," he warned.

"The kicker has to kick-back," we chuckled together. In 1965, Bears icon Mike Ditka had publicly said about Halas, "He throws quarters around like they're manhole covers."

Equally as important was Randy's introduction to George Allen, the Bears defensive coordinator. Allen held the position when the Bears had won a championship. Allen bantered with Randy, but let what would be my new key selling point to create competition for Randy's draft position slip out. "Randy truly displayed the ability and potential on tape in the Michigan State game. That was a top-tier talent performance," Allen emphasized.

In that game Randy played both ways. Nonetheless, he dominated one of college football's premier defensive talents, Bubba Smith. I spread Allen's nugget as fast as one could in 1966 and pointed it out on every inquiring phone call.

Randy soon told Buck he would not sign with the Bears. He sugarcoated it by saying he "always wanted to live by the ocean" and suggested, "the Los Angeles Rams or Baltimore Colts."

Gil Brandt called and before I could hype him, the Dallas Cowboys General Manager spoke and told me he'd seen all of Randy's game tapes. He added, "I am offering the Cowboys 1st round choice."

"It's 23rd or 24th," I exclaimed positively.

"You're doing your homework," said Brandt. "I guarantee we're going to pick a lineman with that choice."

Buck called and said he was booking the penthouse at the Chicago Inter-Con plus a couple of rooms for our whole family, beginning three days before the draft. I liked that because Bob Dylan would be making his second-ever electric performance that weekend at the Erie Crown Theater. "We'll come, Buck, if you get us tickets for the Bob Dylan concert."

"What is a Bob Dylan?" Buck asked, then quickly added, "Done deal... How's about 20 tickets?"

"You're the man, Buck," I shouted enthusiastically, adding, "Buck, we'll need to rent more rooms for those 20 friends to stay in..."

Buck questioned firmly, "Let me get the rest of the Penthouse Floor... because this will be one BIG welcome NFL spectacular... right?"

Our college buddies, girlfriends, football players, and more girlfriends started heading through the Midwestern winter's cold for the even more bitter winds of Chicago. We took over the penthouse floor.

The day before the draft, Buck came into our hotel suite with the good news and the bad news. He was able to get a reservation for everyone at one of Chicago's top swank restaurants, but no Dylan tickets. Buck said, "All they say is he's a dirty, hippie, pinko that can't sing and he still sold out!"

I cut him short, "Buck, the only reason we are in freezing Chicago and not with the New York Jets in THE BAHAMAS ... are those tickets. We are out of here."

I went directly to the phone and called Jets' Tom and said Randy and I plus two girlfriends were ready to meet him in the Bahamas.

"I'll call the Jets travel office and make plane reservations, say in two-three hours." Tom barked.

"Give me ninety minutes," Buck paced and begged. He swore to go to the end of the goddamn earth to get the Dylan tickets.

I said, "In ninety minutes there'll be a taxi taking us to the airport. If you're late, take your friends to the show because I think Dylan's gonna be the artist of my generation."

Buck was back in an hour. From behind his back he whipped out and fanned like a geisha a fistful of tickets. "All row three, center section... and know what I said about Dylan being a filthy, beatnik, hippie...? You're sitting close enough to smell his dirty socks!"

I called Tom and said, "Cancel the Bahamas, but Randy has agreed to sign with the Jets as a tight end for $225,000 spread over 4 years, with 50 thou as the signing bonus."

Ten minutes later Tom called back: "You got a deal."

Bob Dylan performed "The Times They Are A-Changin'" and "Masters of War." He ended the ten-song set with "Chimes of Freedom." A stool with a bottle of water on it was Dylan's total staging for his acoustic performance. This was a man from a small, remote American town that evolved into an artist with an awareness of the world's nihilistic politics.

Dylan, the young troubadour, could communicate that vision and raise consciousness about it. It was a passionate, brilliant performance for an emotionally charged and captivated audience; except for a few. Some of those few, my guests, were all over me during the intermission. Succinctly put, it was, "Who and what was that croakin', couldn't understand what he was singin' about, piece of crap!"

Bob Dylan and Robbie Robertston
Photos: Suki Hill

Those unappreciative few, my friends, exited to the Army-Navy TV highlights back at the hotel. My emphatic, "Dylan's gonna play rock... electric with a band... they're called The Hawks, and they're the best rock band in Canada," could not deter

77

their hasty, grumbling exit to the Inter-Con Hotel.

Dylan returned for second set backed by The Hawks and raced out rockin' with "Tombstone Blues." In the moment after the applause at the song's conclusion, and while the band's lead guitarist, Robbie Robertson, made a minor adjustment to his instrument, a smattering of boos came from a section stage left and far behind our seats. Dylan turned away from the microphone and snapped off a bitter epitaph. The band shared a knowing, 'it will be all right in a minute' with laughs and nods. "Subterranean Homesick Blues" followed Dylan's angry aside. Dylan snarled the song like a streetwise tough. It exhibited a Dylan hardened by life in New York City. His songs also presented that aspect of raw music shared with the blues; the lyrics could be about how rough life really is but lifted you up nonetheless. Three flashing lights and a broad, intermittent spotlight embraced a low-key, rock-and-roll feel.

I knew, from my deep familiarity with Dylan's folk lyrics, that this transitional performance I just witnessed was seminal artistically. I left thrilled and floating on air.

After the concert I was confronted in the lobby of the Inter-Con by the night manager. He was angry and blunt, "No more liquor from room service."

On the penthouse floor the party was raging. My parents were terrified and confined to their room by the revelry. It seemed, they intimated, one or two of the girls may have been entertaining a different male or so in a disgusting display of bed-hopping. I found a different viewpoint standing amongst a room full of half empty liquor bottles and food-filled service carts. One friend or another proclaimed a variation of, "I ordered up a massage and signed a hundred-dollar tip."

Randy was being saluted or roasted by friends at top volume. There was a toast: "Randy, this is a ginormous party!"

Those festivities passed quickly for me, desiring to talk more Dylan set-list, stealth lyrics and the cosmic mind with my friend Bill Wassman and our college friend and early Dylan fanatic, Jackie Horvath. My date Carol and I slipped off with them into one of the hotel rooms and chased "Mr. Tambourine Man," looking for answers that were "Blowing in the Wind."

Draft day came. Randy, soon to be a tight end on the New York Jets by signing a contract in the hotel lobby for a quarter of a million bucks, walked five miles along the frozen shoreline of Lake Michigan to burn off nervous energy. On arrival at the suite, Buck greeted our parents with, "There's quite a bit of social debris staggering around the hall."

Twenty minutes before the NFL draft began, Buck pulled out his ace in the hole. "Randy, you and your parents are going to be on television tonight, on the 5 o'clock news and sports. Yeah, Bruce Roberts, the number one sports broadcaster on Chicago TV, is going to bring two cameras, lights... everything so they can get you on air TONIGHT!"

Of course Randy had to be signed to an NFL team for all of this to occur. Randy and our parents suddenly could think of nothing else. It was as if they were mesmerized and possessed by the thought of being on TV.

Buck offered the by deal, presenting a contract with the numbers typed in. It was for 3 years, totaling $130,000 with $30,000 as a signing bonus. Plus the most fantastic part was Randy would be the fourth pick overall by the Philadelphia Eagles.

Buck threw his arms to the heavens and brayed, "That's why they want to put you on TV... you're the fourth best player in the whole damn country. I'm gonna call Bruce and tell him we're on!"

I called my brother aside and made a passionate appeal that he was throwing away $100,000... the original 'dream amount contract' we had hoped for!

"Not if the league folds," Randy growled loudly, using one of Buck's repeated arguments against the AFL. I would argue back Joe Namath had signed for $400,000 the year before and hadn't missed a paycheck.

It was a bitter blow to me. When two brothers grow up in Gary, Indiana, with all of that City's sudden, constant violence, you're bonded by many life-or-death situations. Most often it was three, four or five against two of us. Surviving those vicious, out-of-the blue attacks meant you had each other's back like no other test except combat.

"You're gonna be a tight end... not down there getting your brains beat in," I pleaded.

"The Jets need a tackle, and so they're lying to get me to sign and then they'll switch me to tackle,"

Randy predicted with a wave.

I countered quickly, as the draft was minutes from starting, "At least go with the Cowboys. They gonna win. I want to see you on a winner... not just three games a year like high school and college. The Eagles are terrible. Their coach has never won anywhere big time."

"I wanna be the fourth guy picked. I wanna be on TV tonight... that's it. You got me all the way to that, Jerry!"

When you grow up the sons of a steel worker and worked summers in the hot, dirty, dangerous steel mills yourselves, it shapes two brothers at 21 and 23 like we were. As teenagers our entire family had survived on three months of dinners on a "Striker's Family Ration" of two hot dogs, three potatoes and four carrots provided by the Union. I didn't want to somehow screw up $130,000 so I shut up.

"So I'm telling Buck if I'm the fourth pick, I'm signing," Randy stated with finality.

I resigned with, "All right, your car is a barely-alive junk. So I'm gonna get you a new car."

"My mother's voice came across the room saying, "The draft's starting... and Buck says your dad and I are going to have to wear makeup to be on TV!"

I interrupted and told Buck, "You gotta throw a new car in there. Every other team offered a new car."

Buck answered, "Jerry, you're outta college, working in the Wrigley Building... a young executive around town... what do you drive?"

"Chevy Super Sport," I boasted, having bought one on a company loan plan.

What I didn't include in my answer was that a few months before, I had volunteered for the Head Start Program. I lived in a veneer mill town where the families at best had running water and outhouses. These dollar-an-hour workers lived in a "one job town" of Edinboro for generations.

I bunked in the guest room of the Baptist preacher who also ran the program with his wife. Like the workers I bought canned noodle soup, beans, and sloppy joe mix at the company store. The owner of the veneer mill had a true mansion on the hill. The manager lived halfway down the hillside, while the workers lived in rough cabins or airstream trailers.

No one spoke to me unless they had to. So I stayed to the task of trying to do something good; and I did.

I unrelentingly pushed for and finally got the small, eight box, variety pack of cereals that was the staple of the college kid morning diet. The company store sold molasses and fried dough, which was the hamlet's breakfast. The breakfast was a key element to giving the Head Start boost in life to the children. I was happy to establish that bit of nutrition before I fulfilled my three-month obligation. I bid the pastor and his wife a sincere wish to finally rid the children of Edinboro of the scourge of scabies and impetigo. I was equally as happy when I grabbed my stack of books and transistor radio and left the poorest white people I'd ever seen in my rearview mirror.

It also made me take the job in public relations, as I had seen the other side.

"Get him a Super Sport and he signs, Buck," I said firmly in my most Public Relations voice.

Buck went to the phone as the first choice in the draft was selected. "I want a Chevy Super Sport for..." Buck spelled out my brother's name... "that can be picked up by him tomorrow." The new car was confirmed in less than a minute.

My brother was picked by the Eagles and signed. He was on the Chicago nightly news and was asked what it felt like to be picked fourth out of nowhere?

My parents' interview made the cutting-room floor. The Cowboys picked a lineman; the Cowboys would appear in 18 playoff games from the late 60's through the early 70's. The Jets picked a lineman; the Jets did develop the tight-end as a down field threat which contributed to their Super Bowl victory, led by Namath. One player held out and didn't sign on draft day, crashing into the 4th round in

HE'S TICKLISH — The three top draft choices of the Philadelphia Eagles gag it up with team physician Dr. James Nixon Saturday. Getting physicals are (left to right): Randy Beisler, 247-pound defensive end from Indiana and Gary Wirt; Gary Pettigrew, 245-pound defensive end from Stanford, and Ben Hawkins, 175-pound flanker back from Arizona State. Also in the photo is Jerry Mazzanti, 240-pound defensive end from Arkansas, who recently returned from the Armed Forces. (AP Wirephoto)

both leagues. When he did sign 10 days later, he got $150,000 more than any player in the draft.

Also on the Eagles was Jim Ringo, who later retired holding the "most consecutive games played" record. Ringo is remembered for the quote of perhaps football's most famous coach, Vince Lombardi. Ringo told Lombardi that an agent would negotiate his contract. "Tell your agent you've been traded to Buffalo," Lombardi said as he picked up the phone and initiated the trade in front of Ringo.

I barely had time to reflect on pro football baby sitters, or the psychological need of humans to be on television, or to hope that Bob Dylan would make an electric album, when another draft notice to kill or be killed in Vietnam arrived. Fortunately I was declared ineligible from an old basketball knee injury. My brother was declared unfit 4-F before he ever played a game in his 11-year NFL career.

RANDY BEISLER

I never took any money from my brother. After Randy's first season with the pathetic, last-place, Eagles football organization, I started thinking about trying to get him traded to another team.

Chapter Twenty

The best jobs are coroner and mortician.
The worst that can happen is you find a pulse.

—Dennis Miller

An offer to be a substitute teacher filled
the immediate need of no-more-school-days life.
I replaced a lady who taught physical science to
15-year-olds. What began as a two week medical
leave changed to a serious medical situation. I was
signed on as a full-time substitute for the rest of the
semester.

Two things were good for me: a sub made *more*
money than a teacher. Two, I could learn a day ahead
of the students because I knew little about rocks,
faults, glaciers and friction in any scholarly way.

Of course, unlike the teachers, I did not get
vacation pay for Spring Break. Didn't matter; school
days for me might be over but one more run with
the wild while I still qualified as a college guy, and
not some long out-of-school loser going down to
prey on the hopelessly drunk. My brother and I had
gone to Daytona Beach and had a lot of fun that was
tempered, for me, by an unseemly side to that much
alcohol.

I was meeting Sally Pierce, a wonderful woman
I had never spent much time around in high school.
We had something going on and I agreed to meet her
in Nassau, Bahamas, and we did. The Bahamas for

Spring Break was little known but had just the right mix of kids from a wide swath of schools, plus The

The Mighty Sparrow

Mighty Sparrow and his island music that says, "You're gonna sweat... you're gonna dance." It was sensational every night they played.

At school after the Break, things got weird. I, being new, was universally warned and prodded by the teachers never, ever to ask a question at the obligatory teachers' meetings. I understood, but now simpleton questions were being asked and an hour of angry, getting hungrier, simpleton answers were being fought over. Previously I had enjoyed the students and the job; I was considering teaching as a viable career.

So I started asking others in the profession and it was unanimous that required teachers' meetings always eventually became sheer hell. I ruled out teaching.

It was the last teacher's meeting of the year, three days before school was out for summer, that was the nail in the coffin.

"Any questions?" the principal asked.

"How come Jerry has gotten paid *more money* than us?"

It caused quite a stir of amplified voices all

around me—one saying, "Who cares, can we get out of here?"

I waited until it died down and said, 'I, being a sub, didn't get paid for Spring Break."

A brief cacophony of replies flew around the room. I threw my hands in the air, turned for the door, and heard, "It didn't keep you from going to the Bahamas."

Chapter Twenty-One

Everyone would meet at Ben Franks and Pandora's Box.
That was a very important corner.

—Mike Nesmith, The Monkees

The Summer of Love began for Bill Wassman and me in December 1966, because on the day we moved into the Old Town district of Chicago—a blizzard! 32 inches of snow fell by move-in night. The main positive result was meeting all of our neighbors in a cold, distant, big city. Wassman had made substantial money in NYC working for major fashion photographers in set lighting. Vista was a Federal program for disadvantaged teenagers. You could do Vista instead of Vietnam. Ironically, the neighborhood Wassman worked in was known in Chicago as the War Zone.

I had sublet Wassman's and his fiancée Patty's New York City 8th floor walk-up at 222 Thomson Street. The streets around there were threatening but Wassman was used to it: he had been arrested and spent three days in the Bastille Prison for a drunken confrontation with French gendarmes on Bastille Day.

His fiancée worked at TWA as a stewardess. An IU grad, she had previously taken a job as a cocktail waitress at Max's Kansas City, so they would have access to all the shows at the underground club du jour. I got to see The Velvet Underground with Nico with Patty's guest pass. A real highlight.

As so was the music in Chicago in 1967. A club opened on Wells Street—the commercial strip through the Old Town District—called Mother Blues. Since it was no longer safe to hit the Southside for the Blues, they were now happily a half mile away: John Lee Hooker, Jimmy Reed, Muddy or the Wolf performed weekly. The nine-piece outfit Chicago brought their brassy, tight rock to Barnaby's at least 3 weekends of 4. Even the local saloon O'Rourke's had *only* the Rolling Stones and Bob Dylan on the jukebox.

The Mole Hole was the first and likely only "head shop" in the Midwest. Rolling papers, pipes and *The Seed*, Chicago's underground newspaper, every bit as politically scathing as *The Berkeley Barb* and the *LA Free Press* were on the West Coast. There was a nice art gallery a block to the south, Jay's Liquors a couple doors down from a hip clothing store, and a terrific jazz club a block to the north, where I saw the greats: Ahmad Jamal, Cannonball Adderley, Wes Montgomery and Jimmy Smith were once-a-month in rotation.

Patty took the TWA job because the airline used Chicago as a primary hub, so she could get days off frequently and see Bill. We all anticipated seeing Big Brother and the Holding Company at Mother Blues. I had seen them in San Francisco. I, like everyone, was overwhelmed by Janis Joplin's voice and stage presentation. The whole neighborhood was buzzing with anticipation.

Outside the Mole Hole on Wells Street the day of the show, I met Sam Andrews, guitarist for Big

Brother. He was lost. "You know how I can find a club... Mother Blues?" he asked me.

"You're Sam Andrews... I'm gonna see the band tonight. I saw you in San Fran... couple months ago."

"That is nice to hear," Andrews said.

"I'll walk you partway. It's about 4 blocks away."

"Much appreciated," Andrews said genuinely.

I ruined the show for everyone in that short walk. "I bought your new album and am gettin' into it," I said innocently.

"What new album?" Andrews stopped and asked.

"You know, *Down on Me*... It's on Mainstream Records."

"Almighty Hell," Andrews said. "Those are demos. Our real album is coming out in three months," he exclaimed, adding loudly, "Those are stolen demos... unfinished! That son of a bitch Bob Chadd I bet."

It seemed Chadd had done the songs in December and released the single "Blind Man/All is Loneliness" to no public reception, but after the band's wild success at the Monterey Pop Festival had rushed the slapdash album out.

"I had no idea," I said. "It's right there in the record store... Featured!" Before I knew it we were at the club, Andrews plotting revenge.

Janis Joplin broke down when he told her. It showed early in the band's performance when she started crying and talking, "Lowlife, piece of shit, ripoffs..." After a few half-hearted songs: "I'm gonna go backstage and pull myself together," Joplin told the befuddled crowd, "and come back out here and kick ass for you." She never came back out.

Chapter Twenty-Two

Being perfectly well-dressed gives a feeling of tranquility
that religion is powerless to bestow.

—Ralph Waldo Emerson

An agency supplied cars for people who had moved great distances and did not want to drive to their new location. My car was now cash. I packed my best suit and tie and drove a hard 48 hours so I would get extra use of the car to relocate myself. When I arrived in San Francisco, I took the first good job I could find that came with a company car, since I had no money for one. Strasenburgh Laboratories hired me, and a Plymouth with 2000 miles on it came from the regional representative I was replacing.

I had no idea that Strasenburgh's number- one selling product was B-phetamine, which allowed brand distance from the "ooh, bad" amphetamine. The "B" stood for buffer, allegedly to soothe the stomach.

It was in demand. I would attend conferences anywhere between Palo Alto and San Francisco, my territory, where doctors and other pharmaceutical reps asked for extra samples. Attempts at *buying* the samples came

STRASENBURGH LABORATORIES
ROCHESTER, NEW YORK, U.S.A., DIV. WALLACE & TIERNAN INC.

GERALD W. BEISLER
Medical Sales Representative

1711 LEAVENWORTH STREET
SAN FRANCISCO, CALIFORNIA 94129
PHONE: 474-3395

from the other reps.

Life magazine did an exposé as the feature article on how many overweight women were dying from using not only Strasenburgh's pills but their competitors', who used a slightly different formula with the same results.

I never went to work again, figuring they would be firing me. My territory of course was one of the wealthiest in the US. So two months later, without me, I was representative of the month!

I drove that company car for three more months until I appeared in a *San Francisco Chronicle* photo with the Diggers, in a feature article on the emerging "hippie" culture. I was there by accident as the Diggers finished their free food give-away.

Automatically, I offered my supervisor the truthful defense that I had wandered up to the free food gathering because I was lost.

"Just being *that* close to those drug dealers is enough to fire you, and you are," he answered, throwing his arms in the air as he stomped off.

Also, perhaps more importantly, there were the complaints to company headquarters about "lack of samples" available in my territory.

Chapter Twenty-Three

*We must believe in luck. For how can we explain
the success of those we don't like?*

—Jean Cocteau

One of the major benefits of attending San
Francisco State was the open, cordial mingle in the
Student Union with exchange students from Ghana,
Morocco, various South American countries, Kenya
and England. The knowledge, history, geography and
politics were shared openly with boots-on-the-ground
sources.

We all awaited Bobby Seale, Party Chairman
of the Black Panther Party. He was addressing to the
students and faculty as part of the Black Arts and
Culture lecture series.

The Black Panthers were held in high esteem
on campus because they had used the university's
campus green to feed 500 children breakfast, a
worthwhile program that had been ended due to a
bureaucratic no-no. The school had given the student
book store management to the Black Students Union
who operated it in the same enthusiastic manner it had
previously functioned.

I, of course, came out of Gary, Indiana where
I never felt a hint of racism. I participated in three
sports against all the Gary schools in sports and some
were all African American. From the 3rd grade until
graduation I never felt a twinge of racism from a

player, referee, coach or parent at any of these athletic competitions. I went everywhere and anywhere in the city. In 1962 Gary elected the first Black mayor of a city with a population of 250,000 or more. So I was an eyewitness to the change from a blissful access to Gary's many cross-cultural attractions.

Everything had changed for the worst sadly. These few years later it seemed as if rich people, movie stars and international athletes were integrated but not the middle class. With the Vietnam War raging it was easy to accept the Panthers' black berets, leather jackets and militant edge.

Seale addressed the college crowd with a snarl and repeatedly called the police "pigs." He used the derogatory "honkies" for whites in attendance. He said, "If we were to unify it would be around guns." The only profound thing Seale said, "Politics begins with an empty stomach," was lost in more statements like, "The only answer to white brutalization is guns and force."

I ran into Ali the Moroccan exchange student on the way out. "I come from a monarchy, and Seale wouldn't be walking around already!" he said, snapping his fingers for emphasis.

Chapter Twenty-Four

I'm young and able to buzz all night long. I'm a king bee.

—Slim Harpo

A hit TV show about teenagers had a blond, doofus male, Dobie Gillis, and a homely, extremely intelligent female that was Dobie's foil. There was a beautiful, coiffed up, blonde girl and Maynard G. Krebs. Krebs was an adolescent Beatnik who espoused a few generalized ideas from Beatnik culture that permeated into TV in a goofy way.

Joe Fish was my high school's Beatnik. It made him the school weirdo and outcast. Through music we bonded. The school weirdo played jazz for me in his family's basement. He got out of town fast to Austin, Texas. We re-introduced ourselves in the Armadillo World headquarters and it would lead to two important connections. Texas Tom and Texas Jim, purveyors of the absolute, most in-demand Mexican cannabis. And thus my entrée into so very many things.

Chet Helms was another Texan now relocating to and opening the Avalon Ballroom in San Francisco.

Joe Fish became Little Joe and the Lights how doing many nights of backup lighting and were credited on many of the Venue's artistic promotion posters.

I had the run of the place. The cannabis was euphoric but more importantly inspirational.

Musicians especially loved it for that reason. I watched the greats smoke, grab their instrument, or write a few lines they "had been looking for" and also work on coming up with new guitar tunings. David Crosby would get obsessed with the new tunings for a burst of ten to fifteen minutes after a joint.

Chet Helms was agonizing when I walked into his quasi-office. "Look," he pointed at a *Rolling Stone* magazine. "It says guys like me and the white musicians have given nothing back to early, black artists that created Rock and Roll." He exclaimed that, "I have sent money to the main booker in Chicago twice and never got anything but ripped off."

It led to a great musical success for me. "You send the money to Sam Lacey Booking?" I asked Helms.

"How you know that?" he answered.

"I have a personal rapport with him... I did a successful show with him in the past. Let me handle the nights and it'll be good. I'll get Steve Miller to play too. He'll be happy... very happy to play with one of those Chicago blues legends."

"Two nights?" the always genial Helms asked.

"Can't bring these old guys that far for one night and the Avalon will *need* two nights for ticket demand!"

"What you get out of it?" Helms queried as he began to roll what I hoped was an agreement joint of some sort.

"I get to see an 'All-Time' night. Muddy Waters might jam with Steve Miller... that kinda thing. It will be super great! Plus I'll bring Susie Q one night and Little Latin Lupe Lu the other."

It was. The Howlin' Wolf opened for Steve Miller for two sold-out shows July and 12, 13, 14. Feeling it was very, very rare that San Francisco was real hot at night but both nights were maybe 90°.

My first overriding experience in the warm glow of the backstage that indicates the participants felt it was special was a long, thank-you bear hug from a sweating-through-every-stitch-of-his-clothes Howlin' Wolf.

"You were fantastic," I gasped from inside the human sauna. "Like always..."

"It was slick man... Get me a gig with Eric Clapton, will ya?"

The promo poster indicated the Wolf would play a third night. The Wolf played the first two. Sam Lacey told me by phone, "The Wolf's fat ass is on a plane back to Chicago... Two nights is all you deserve."

Chapter Twenty-Five

The President has got this war
No one knows what the killin' for
Ask the cause or give a reason
They turn it around and call it treason

—Les McCann, "Make It Real Compared to What?"

Tear gas choked the anti-war demonstrators on the commons at San Francisco State. The San Francisco police were using their batons violently. When I saw my classmate K.O. Hallinan catch one right in the face I headed for the parking lot and safety.

There was a *San Francisco Chronicle* van parked a slot or two away and a reporter and cameraman were running from the melee behind me. "I got the shot of that student with his face busted up!" the photographer shouted across the roof of the van, as he quickly jumped into the passenger seat.

A half hour later I had crossed the Golden Gate Bridge on my way home. When I hit the city streets two police cars pulled me over.

"You still stink like tear gas, hippie... Gimme your license," said one cop with his hand on his gun.

"Hands on the roof and assume the position," ordered the other officer.

They went through the car and trunk thoroughly for a half hour without finding marijuana, as their back-and-forth barking indicated they were after.

In my jacket pocket, where I frequently carried a joint, they found some flakes and proudly announced I was under felony arrest for possession. They put the handcuffs on me, called a tow truck and pushed me in one of the police cars. On the way to jail the officers made it quite clear I was guilty of treason.

My girlfriend Yoshiko bailed me out the following morning and we stopped for breakfast at a favorite mom-and-pop cafe. I bought the morning *Chronicle*, and as the old media adage states, "If it bleeds it leads": there was K.O. Hallinan's face gushing blood on the front page.

I knew Tony Serra fought cannabis cases hard and won most of the time. I went to his office and asked him to represent me. Serra said, "You're charged with possession of seven one-hundredths of a gram. It's a one-to-ten felony. I'll take your case *pro bono* if you'll let me take it to the Supreme Court. Seven one-hundredths of a gram is the one to expose how stupid this law is."

I agreed.

Serra added, "I'll find a young lawyer to set the date for your court case; I'll do the trial."

I agreed.

Yoshiko was with me when I met the two lawyers fresh out of law school. "You're the second case we have handled in our new legal partnership."

"I hope so," Yoshiko whispered to me sincerely. "'Cause that's a skunk and a drunk."

"They don't do much but agree on the time," I comforted her.

The Skunk and the Drunk came to the trial to observe Serra's presentation. A clerk brought out a very large manila envelope with block letters angled across the front. EVIDENCE, it read. Judge Roth opened it and peered inside. "Did you bring the proper file?" he asked the clerk.

Before the clerk could reply, the prosecutor rose and stated, "Look again, Your Honor... there's seven one-hundredths of a gram."

Judge Roth flipped the evidence folder, tapped his desk with both hands, and looked at Serra. No one said a word until the prosecutor stood again and stammered, "The people wish to drop the charges, Your Honor."

There went my Supreme Court case.

Chapter Twenty-Six

The USA is like the guy that gives cocaine to everyone
at the party and still nobody likes him.

—Jim Samuels

"Baby, you made love like you just out of prison... not one night in jail." Yoshiko laughed lightly and purred.

It was one of the last sweet things she would say to me. She had gotten the bail money from her parents, explaining in the moment that my arrest was San Francisco State-related.

Then her parents tied the riot to the cannabis bust as a linear "political" operation.

Yoshiko's parents were hidden as Chinese in Seattle during the Internment of ethnic Japanese in California. Their relatives there had been "rounded up," I learned, as they stated why their daughter was never going to see me again.

At the time, the generation gap was so strong that it seemed half the youth in the anti-war/peace movement were from somewhere else. "How long it had been since you talked to someone in your family" crept into conversations. An open counter-culture revolution was in full swing.

A few mumbled this-and-thats, and Yoshiko standing straight with no smile; silent.

"I understand..." I turned to leave.

Yoshiko said the last words she would say to

me. "Jerry, please show up in court so my parents don't lose the bail bond."

"It already cost me you. My date can't happen *soon* enough," I replied with a certain confidence, as I counted up the years in my head. The Internment was less than 30 years ago. I grokked it.

Chapter Twenty-Seven

Living with a saint is more grueling than being one.

—Robert Neville

What I at first felt was, "Wow, this is a true witchy woman." The mantic arts in her view were physic, astrology, tarot, Native American spirit animal, the Chinese calendar, and...

There was never a deviation from that point of view for today's activities, tomorrow's promise, and "Today's tarot card is the Ace of Cups and that means..."

There's important trade-offs early in a new relationship. I gave it lip service for big, warm, wet kisses. I can manage that and pull *some* knowledge out of it.

I had just taken two suitcases of cannabis to Chicago, mainly to go with the old friends to see The Doors. It had been lucrative enough; when Witchy said, "We should go to Popayan, Colombia. It is a physic vortex. That is the nearest," I could say,

"OK?"

We boarded a small prop airplane whose logo, painted on the tail, was the cartoon creatures Hekel and Jekel. We landed in Meddain and grabbed a nice luxury bus up to Popayan.

"You'll be staying at the Hotel Monasterio, I assume?" asked a passenger on the bus, adding, "I'm American Peace Corps. My wife teaches English there."

"Does the Monasterio have good food?" I queried.

"The Monasterio has a French chef, a Chilean wine list and a spring-fed swimming pool."

And it did.

Witchy had said it was a day of days to travel and in one smooth day we made it from San Francisco to a gourmet dinner in one of the world's physic vortexes! We smoked a joint I had brought to many of my compliments, acknowledging her manifestation was reality.

It was a beautiful morning in the Andes when I asked, not thinking of any of the mantic arts, "Where do you think I could hunt up some pot-o-rama?"

"There." She pointed at three crosses that are traditional and found widely in the Hispanic world.

We followed a path to the top of the hill and were enjoying the view of the architecture of the thousand-year-old colonial town, when a young man appeared from the path up the other side of the hill.

Possibly it was the influence of the three crosses but he looked remarkably like Jesus. The beard, the hair, the magnetic eyes were right out of a painting or illustration of the prophet. He said he had come from Ecuador in every manner of transport over three months.

"You know where I can get some smoke?" I asked, traveler to traveler.

"I can *give* you some for a few days' supply... halfway here from Ecuador they grow a lot of it. I've got some red type and a golden. A farmer gave me the gold stuff and it's killer."

Every moment in Popayan was magical. We caught two local flamenco guitarists that had played together once a month in the town plaza for 40 years. A daily dip in a world-class pool, a convivial dinner with the Peace Corps member and his wife. He too laid a surprise bag of local cannabis on me.

When Witchy told his wife how much fun we were having, she said, "It's almost a honeymoon before the *real* honeymoon."

That was not to be. In fact, 72 hours after returning to California we flamed out.

Witchy said, "That card is the Hanged Man. It means the death of *something* today."

Chapter Twenty-Eight

If society wants me to be an outlaw,
then I'll be an outlaw and a damned good one.
That's something people need.
People at all times need outlaws.

—Ken Kesey

Sausalito represented the very best of the arts: great food, good Mary Jane, and easy sex. The Trident Restaurant was where all came together, including movie stars--not old studio system hacks but emerging stars of "New Wave"--and emerging rock stars like Grace Slick, David Crosby, and Bob Weir. My access to the finest cannabis was my passport to enter the buzz and pizzazz. Plus, the owner Frank Werber and I hit it off after he realized I'd seen The Kingston Trio, Lime Lighters, and Joan Baez live, as his fame came from success in the folk music genre.

The star of the show was Confetti Eddie. Everyone swarmed him like a long-lost love because he flew the best Mary Jane in from Mexico, and as a result threw money around like confetti.

Eventually our paths crossed, and I learned he had just pulled it off again, as evidenced by every female at the bar enjoying a drink he had bought. Eddie said, "I only fly 50 to 100 damn miles... There are small airstrips scattered on each side of the border. Just off-the-books biz that everybody knows about."

He looked nonplussed. "Gotta change the strips, 'cause there's plenty of thieving white bread on one side and *mucho banditos* the other. The good thing is both scumbags go for the before-and-after delivery *vehicles*. I've had more hops cancelled 'cause it was ripped off on the way to the strip! Learn how to fly and I'll hook you up, buckaroo."

Gnoss Field in Marin County had the shortest runway of any municipal airport in the country. It was surrounded by wetlands and had a high-stress wind that came over the coastal hills directly from the Pacific and took one by surprise. Learning to fly under

the toughest conditions would be a benefit, a sentiment shared by the instructor for my first lesson a few days later. I flew my first solo flight to Sacramento International Airport within two weeks.

When I told Confetti Eddie that, he was impressed, and shortly after introduced me to the powers that be. I made one hop and though it went smooth, it was white-knuckle scary and enough for me. Not to mention the realization that I had never learned to navigate--I was just following highways and train tracks. The suspense of what was waiting at the other end was fortunately not much. Waiting were two guys that handed me *my* green and handled the green cargo with great care. Plus Confetti Eddie, to fly the plane back to Mexico with boxes of "tax-free electronic shit."

"I'll see you at the Trident," I said, with a let's-get-going wave.

"Hey," Confetti Eddie yelled out of the cockpit, "you went from buckaroo, which is a can-do guy with *huevos,* to a buccaneer, which is can-do, *huevos* and some kind or other brains!"

I never saw Confetti Eddie again.

Chapter Twenty-Nine

The world would not be in such a snarl if Marx would have been Groucho instead of Karl.

—Irving Berlin

Big Red Ted came back from two years in an impoverished corner of Southern India as a member of the Peace Corps, wearing a dhoti, sandals and shoulder-length hair. I was glad to see him as I considered him one of the few guys who played football with my brother that was a bit worldly and unlike a number of players, who jumped into action in Viet-Nam. Big Red Ted had been an exchange student to Moscow which I gave great credit, sharing a broader worldview while in school together.

He had been kicked off the IU football team for accidentally discharging a double-barrelled shotgun while drunk and blowing half the roof off a car he was riding in, driven by another football players.

There he was, standing in my apartment door, skinny and soft-spoken in the all-white, simple cloth outfit, nowhere near the scholarly, happy, wild-man party animal. We caught up on two years of stories; my time in the Headstart program, the Summer of Love, and what it was like digging irrigation ditches in a dusty village where Ted could only speak English to one person. Also Ted promised some rare, hashish pleasure, as he had shipped some fantastic hash to his waiting lady-love back in Indiana, saying he would move to San Francisco with her and the smoke within weeks.

For now he begged for one thing: a swim. "I barely saw anything as big as a mud puddle for two years in the Indian desert," in the village he'd been assigned to.

It was April and the only place I had ever heard of where the water temperature might just be warm enough for swimming was Lake Anza, tucked in the back of the Berkeley hills. We went and joined a couple dozen Berkeley students and hippies enjoying a quick, cool dip or two.

Suddenly there was a hubbub that turned into an outcry: they're ripping off People's Park! All I knew of People's Park was that hippies had transformed a long-vacant, garbage-strewn chunk of land into gardens and a park near the Telegraph Avenue corner of Berkeley, voluntarily making it into a pristine urban oasis.

Photo: Ron Alexander

We went to see what was going on but could not get near the

113

Telegraph area. Parking two miles away, we were both shocked at what we encountered on foot. Downtown Berkeley was on fire. Police cars, people popping out of nowhere wearing bandanas across their mouths, combating a torrent of tear gas while firing rocks at the cops. It conjured images of the racially-based riots the country had been experiencing. Through my tear-gas watery eyes, I could see the Bank of America in flames. We carefully circled out of the violence and back to the car.

It was hard for me to fathom that the "B" actor joke on the door of the lifeguard dressing room door was Governor of California, but right on fake tough-guy cue, Ronald Reagan threw gas on the fire with, "If they want a blood bath, I'll give them a blood bath." The next day, Big Red Ted went to collect his sweetheart and the gooey, sticky hash.

I would participate in the big save-the-park demonstration, most notably documented by flower-bearing hippies nose-to-nose with the National Guard bayonets.

Ted and his girlfriend were busted on a host of charges for hashish smuggling. Both took a jail-free but very severe plea deal.

In six weeks Big Red Ted returned to California, hair shorn, slacks and sport coat, married to another woman who was obviously quite wealthy. Ted blamed his arrest on his previous girlfriend.

I didn't know if it was some form of self-examination but in the first few conversations we had, he seemed to be always praising his old teammate, my brother, and being highly desirous of toking with him to share the glory days of football past. Each time, I told him my brother had two kids now and still had never *tried* cannabis.

"You were the wild, crazy guy on that team," I would say, "And he doesn't have more than a beer these days." I would add, "I have tried LSD, mescaline, and psilocybin... all of which have shown the oneness between people, nature and spirituality. You'll like the new perspective."

"Keep three things in mind, man," he would reply. "The wife would divorce me... Money gone... Nose-to-nose with the bayonets. I'm on heavy-duty probation and can only smoke a joint here and there... so I'm on Marlboros and stinky-breath-free vodka."

Chapter Thirty

Even when Ivan the Terrible had someone executed, he would spend a long time in repentance and prayer. God placed this burden on him. He should have been more decisive.

—Joseph Stalin

I had to get my brother off the Philadelphia Eagles and out to California. The Eagles were a losing, dysfunctional organization with no hope in sight to my trained football eye. I had been extolling California and telling him I was moving there since I was a teenager. I got a meeting with Tony Morabito, the organizationally all-powerful person at the San Francisco 49ers. Two sisters who knew little about football had inherited the team so they put the team in Morabito's absolute control.

He heard my suggestion that he trade for my brother like he was doing me a big favor. "When I talked to you on the phone, I didn't know you were this young," he said with disgust.

I blurted that my brother had put on 35 pounds muscle and still had his speed... married with kids... played offensive and defensive end for the Eagles...

"Ok, I got it." Curtly and firmly he pointed me to the door.

As I left I said the only thing I had cooked up, "I just want him in California away from all that violence back East... so I'll try Al Davis too."

Oakland Raiders headquarters was a helter-skelter operation. Scouts, injured players on crutches or with a cast on an arm, doctors, and position coaches scurried by as I waited my obligatory hour and a half.

"Mr. Davis will see you now."

Al Davis didn't get up but motioned me to a chair across the room.

"As I said in my phone call, sir, I would like to have you entertain the idea of trading for my brother, who has gained 35 pounds of muscle mass and lost no speed in his three years with the Eagles... he's one of if not the fastest lineman in the NFL." Then I got inspired. "All the reports back in college even said he has a mean streak."

"Married?"

"Kids!" I emphasized.

"I'll get a look at our scouting reports on him. Thanks for his and your desire to relocate to California. I'll call *you*," he finished.

"I strongly wanted him to be a Raider when he was drafted and I spoke with some Raider official twice. He *wanted* to be a Raider," I said as I got up.

"I'm gonna tell you somethin' good," Al Davis said from across his desk. "You don't wear a watch. You're not a slave to time, that's good. Because it's about projects and not time. Look--" he held up his arm, exposing a large, shiny, silver, jewel-encrusted watch and band. "It doesn't work, kiddo. Now get the fuck outta here."

I called the 49ers and got Morabito's secretary. I asked if she remembered me and when she confirmed it readily, I asked her to tell Mr. Morabito that Al Davis liked my pitch.

Randy Beisler became a 49er in days, if not hours.

He would soon play for them during the end of a meaningless exhibition game against the Oakland Raiders. On the last play of the game, a Raider sucker-punched my brother in the throat and brought him to his knees. "That was from Al," he shouted into my brother's helmet earhole. The lowlife would never play another snap in the National Football League: gone with a hundred other players in a "mandatory cut" the following day.

Chapter Thirty-One

If you're lost in the woods, play Solitaire.
Someone is sure to show up and tell you to play
the red jack on the black queen.

—Unknown

In Valencia, Spain, the moon landing is on a small black-and-white TV high in the corner of an oceanside cafe. In broken English from behind a counter, the owner is screaming at an American couple and Gomez from Oakland, my traveling partner.

"Americans... The moon... *Muy grande...* American kill the baby in Vietnam!" Gomez had stood close and in front of the TV while excitedly translating some of the Spanish language coverage.

"Out, out," the owner shouted, "No moon here. No Vietnam here!"

From the beginning of my start south from England, Vietnam was daily more magnified. In youth hostels, sidewalk cafes, and on the trail to Marrakesh. In Amsterdam, a shop sold Canadian flags to put on the back of your backpack. It spared you from the out-of-nowhere-in-your-face screaming banshee, talkin' napalm, or the small stone whistling past your ear in the flea market.

Getting thrown out of the cafe put me on the "next possible" ferry to Morocco. My mission now was to score hashish—and slide a bit a home to enjoy—prized hashish from the Atlas mountains. Plus to obtain the hash from the legendary man with the 'face on his hand.' That tattoo was proof you were getting the very best from the right plantation.

By the time I got to Fez and its Wild West environs I was Morocco knowledgeable. Marrakesh was a great place to learn how the old bazaar, decent food, shelter and operating behind quality keif which was openly used, puffed in local pipes, that was offered two hits at a time. Also worldwide media had given much attention to the Rolling Stones hanging out in Marrakesh, which likely contributed to the bevy of lovely English lasses.

An American couple I joined up with, on a mutual pursuit of Berber jewelry in old Medina, went mindless and paranoid. They were already separated from their guide/taxi driver, and the sun goes behind the mountains, bringing darkness early to the heavily canopied bazaar. He ran this way and she ran that way, both yelling, pleading for the driver. I tried to tell them I had planned on walking out and was confident I knew the way.

Each used a different expletive in front of: "---- idiot, get away from us!"

I started walking out, and a man came out of the shadows. "I'm the man with the face-on-his-hand," he said, holding his arm out and pulling his sleeve back so I could see the tattoo.

"I was looking for you," I said.

"Let us go find some pleasure," he replied.

Chapter Thirty-Two

Love is not the dying moan of a distant violin...
It is the triumphant twang of the bed spring.

—S.J. Perelman

Howard Wales, an extraordinary organ player, and Jelly Roll Troy, a bass player with, as a reviewer called it, the "voice of an angel," were held in high musical esteem by me due to being members of "The Clique," a group of studio musicians in Detroit that backed Mo-Town acts. They also held musical "gravitas" with Mike Bloomfield. The two created this

or that with him but Bloomfield, at the call of Bob Dylan, always left everything and everyone in the lurch.

Jelly Roll was also in a band that toured with the Dick Clark Caravan of Rock and Roll. On Jelly Roll's first tour with

Art by Mancuso

the Caravan, he turned 15 years old. Jerry Garcia
met Jelly two years later at a cannabis dealer to the
"steady, working players."

I met Jerry Garcia through those two and
synched through a shared "love" of music and sharing
a heavy connection to our sources of the finest smoke.
The latter was especially valuable at the time because
of what were called "droughts" of availability as rock
and roll spread the demand across the nation.

One fabulous thing that Garcia and I shared that
manifested on two trips over the mountain to Stinson
Beach was being raised on Broadway musicals.
My parents and Jerry's mom played the LP's of
South Pacific, *Oklahoma*, *West Side Story* and more,
over and over. This would lead to Garcia saying,
"Oklahoma," and me singing to stretch the meaning of
the word,

"Oooooooklahoma, where the wind goes..."
Garcia: "Surrey with the fringe on top,"
followed by a quick, "They call the wind Maria."
Lotta laughin'!
Me: "Here come the Jets like a bat outta Hell."
Garcia: "Maria... I just met a girl named Maria..."

I could remember a verse or two and the chorus,
but Garcia knew all the words to all the songs and
made them his own.

One lyrical suggestion I made to Garcia, as we
hugged the treacherous Mt. Tam curves in my '59
red Porsche en route to my seaside bungalow, was,
"I never got how the pretty girl in 'Ramblin' Rose' is
told to ramble on. A lovely lady like that to Muddy

or Mick would be invited to sit down," I said.

"On their knee," laughed Garcia. "We'll fix that when we record it."

I did have one song I had parodied for years with full-on basso-perfundo, over-the-top, operatic style... "Some Enchanted Evening." I broke it out and he loved it and added that "Some Enchanted Evening" was a romantic guide in his life. I told him I had pulled it out when a date was going well and I was just drunk enough. Nonetheless, I told him, I noticed how the song advanced the moment.

Garcia said, "So you added it to your tool box." He added, "I'm a happily married man with children now, but I can still remember when a song or two came to value movin' the clock and ending up in the bag of tricks. But now I've got daughters and gonna have to warn 'em about some boys like us."

We laughed together as the Pacific Ocean and

123

the first glimpse of the town came into view.

"So with that thought in mind... from *South Pacific*," Garcia chortled, breaking into, "Gonna wash that man right out of my hair... Gonna wash that man right out of my hair..."

Chapter Thirty-Three

*I could steal, rape, and murder with blessings
of the most powerful in the country.*

—Diary of George Hunter White

In a diary published after his death, George
Hunter White describes his second arrest of iconic
vocalist Billie Holiday in a Nob Hill hotel penthouse.
He set Holiday up, having the room service delivery
man supply her with drugs one night. The next night,
White made his excuse for more than an arrest. Two
San Francisco drug agents burst into the room after
White shouted, "You're under arrest for possession of
drugs," and pointed to paraphernalia on the bedside
table.

The detectives handcuffed Holiday and
removed her clothes for a full cavity search. White
then had the detectives handcuff Holiday by only
one arm to the bedpost. White writes how Holiday
predictably acted since she recognized him from
the first bust, "As I thought; naked, she waved her
claws and arm, threatening, snarling like a wild black
panther."

Jerry Garcia and I had no idea a scumbag like
White lived in the beach town of 400 people.

White writes how in a short 10 day period, he
dosed two teenage girls that were daughters of his
wife's friends. He raped one then the other. His wife

remained married to him.

White was using high-end escort girls when he inadvertently dosed a Cabinet-level official in New York City. Unaware he was on LSD, the official thought he had gone crazy. He phoned his wife and told her that before he jumped to his death. They transferred White to San Francisco.

White writes how he set up a large "safe house with a two way mirror" where he could watch and enjoy a bottle a day of gin while he compromised, manipulated and abused people for years.

White writes that for a time he helped perfect Viagra by enticing seamen from foreign vessels to ingest a pill, the woman offering a "freebie." Some of the early dosage was off, causing the veins in the user's penis to explode. When four foreign sailors had that bloody experience quickly one after another, to White's drunken delight, he wrote, "They shouldn't call it a 'sex helper' but a 'sex ender.'"

White had one specific operation that cemented his unbridled power. During World War II, after German sabotage on the NYC docks, Naval Intelligence handled the problem by enlisting the Mafia to run the waterfront. History says Lucky Luciano oversaw 21 top Mafia enforcers that ended the problem. After the war, Thomas Dewey, a District Attorney running as a Republican for President, deported Luciano to Italy. Luciano was living in a beachside luxury villa when White showed up and suggested Luciano give up the 21 men so they be systematically killed, and Luciano could enjoy the rest of his life in the villa. The brevity of this description should not mean the meeting was brief for much is written history of the event. Luciano did put the name to the 21 death warrants.

The old drunken pervert was now down to running operations out of the Stinson Beach Volunteer Fire Department.

Garcia would find out about White's presence in Stinson Beach first of course, being a national anti-Vietnam War figure, pro-cannabis and the image of a born rebel. The Stinson Beach Volunteer Fire Department had become much more than a volunteer firehouse because it is the listening post to watch for submarine possibilities under the Golden Gate Bridge, thus the Fire Chief had to be a Federal employee.

Things had gotten weird, some stuff seemed to be *anticipated* that just gave Garcia a feeling his phone was tapped. He had a parking lot meeting with the Grateful Dead's lawyer, Michael Stepanian. Besides being the Dead's lawyer, Stepanian was the cannabis defense lawyer of reknown equal to Tony Serra and Patrick Hallinan. There was a lot of work for them. Stepanian also wrote a column for *High Times* magazine that revealed the secrets, techniques and ways of defeating the routine lies the prosecution used in cannabis cases.

Stepanian carefully brought in a wire-tap expert from another state. Garcia's phone *was* being tapped and it traced to the Stinson Beach Volunteer Fire Station, the lair of George Hunter White.

Sadly, Garcia would tell me too late to benefit from the knowledge.

ASSOCIATED PRESS

Members of the Grateful Dead faced reporters in San Francisco in 1967, following a police raid on their residence resulting in marijuana possession charges. Shown here are managers Rock Scully, left, and Dan Rifkin; band members Bob Weir and Jerry Garcia; and attorney Michael Stepanion.

Now George Hunter White was standing on my porch with a longnosed .45 caliber gun strapped to his leg with rawhide, à la John Wayne. I saw White's big-brimmed bush hat before Agent James McGunn forced my head down with his pistol to the back of my head—and that can turn an evening around.

Earlier I had sold the Porsche for much-needed capital and checked one last time on Floyd, my cat's, transitioning to another pet guardian. Floyd, a backdoor orphan, had been with me through three apartments and a cabin before the Stinson Beach bungalow. Outdoors all day and indoors all night was Floyd's survival mode. Sitting on his new servant's lap, Floyd heard her say... music to my ears... "This fantastic cat is out all day and in at night, like you said."

"Possession and distribution of counterfeit currency," Agent McGunn said as he handcuffed me.

Bogus Bills Scrub Man's World Trip

A Stinson Beach man, scheduled to leave for an around-the-world trip yesterday, instead spent the day in Marin County Jail waiting for federal authorities.

Gerald W. Beisler, 27, of 2 Francisco Patio, was arrested yesterday on suspicion of passing counterfeit money.

Marin County Sheriff's deputies said Beisler purchased two airline tickets Saturday for around-the-world trips from Talbot Travel Service at Strawberry Town and Country Shopping Center.

He paid $2,830 cash for the tickets, deputies said, but $340 of it turned out to be in phony $20 bills.

U.S. Secret Service agents were called in and arrested Beisler at his home.

At the home, deputies said, Secret Service agents found $3,500 in $100 and $10 bills, all legitimate currency.

Beisler was held at Marin County Jail pending an appearance in federal court in San Francisco.

McGunn searched the bungalow quickly and thoroughly, it sounded like to me. My suitcases were still open as I prepared the dream "buy low, sell high" trip to Asia (with a cool, smart, though very new sweetheart).

"George, there's nothing in sight and no indication these suitcases were *ever* filled with 50k... Your snitch is full of shit and I flew 3000 miles on a Friday!"

"I had *two* saying the same thing. 50k," I heard White answer as I smelled his sickening alcohol breath.

McGunn replied it was foggy and dangerous driving over that mountain tonight, so I'm going up the coast to the first motel available. "You," he said to me, "are going to jail for the weekend for... *let's say*, your past misdeeds."

George Hunter White called for a deputy on his walkie-talkie. Cuffed in the backseat of a Marin Sheriff's vehicle, I had to endure one last blast of putrid breath from the evil White: "Who you think you are, driving that red Porsche around like you own the place?"

Chapter Thirty-Four

The more crap you believe is true the better off you are.

—Charles Bukowski

Tony Serra, attorney-at-law, met me for a pre-organized mouth-to-ear meeting at the noisy No-Name Tavern in Sausalito. He showed me a list of names on a page with his letterhead on it... tore his letterhead off the top of the paper and said, "Keep those names. They are the judge in the case, Zerpole, and three clients of your lawyer, Paul Harris, Michael Zorgen, and Robert Andre. He conned the lawyer community by telling everyone he had won a case overturning the Draft. In fact he merely filed a pleading with Zerpole."

"He told me that same grandiose tale," I answered firmly.

Tony Serra put a hand on my shoulder and said, "He and his partner may not be on your side and your case starts tomorrow. I been busy as hell and I just been putting a few things together with my legal partners and figuring those guys out."

I leaned in and told him, "George Hunter White was with the Federal agent and the Marin deputy that drove me to jail."

"This is a White operation?" Serra stated firmly.

"Oh yeah," I said. "The agent berated White when he didn't find a gazillion dollars that White's informant had told him I had, is what I've come up with."

"More dots connected," Serra said with a nod, adding, "I'm going to walk to the corner, put some money in the parking meter and *think* what to do."

When Serra returned I immediately said, "I'll fire them. Those whatever-they-are *pro bono*."

"Too late," Serra said. "If every defendant could fire their lawyer the day of the trial, half would. The judge won't go for it and they will know you're onto them. Here's what we're gonna do. There's going to be a gentleman there, older, white mustache, and important—a bow tie. He's my eyes and ears. You do anything he says. If I'm wrong about these two disgraces to the legal system, and they have a tiny bit of competence, you still may be done on Day One. You have a Federal agent that came 3000 miles with no reason explained for 300 bucks. He lied and said you were a felon. You have no record. No search warrant. No probable cause. That agent could have asked you at noon instead of 10:30 at night... where you got the money."

"He never asked any of those questions. A real Sherlock Holmes!"

"Now these Federal judges don't like to wrap things up in one day in spite of that. Bow-Tie will tell me if we're just legal-dancing for a second day or the big, big fix is in... You know someone in Washington, D.C. actually thinks you're a traitorous spy for the commies. You were never in the Weathermen, or some fringe politics?"

I told him straight, "I'm trying to end the killing

machine of war now—nonviolently, anything I can contribute. And I want non-hard drugs legalized. And every day my cock has a say in it all."

Serra said, "Listen to Bow-Tie if there's a Day Two."

Chapter Thirty-Five

When he said we were trying to make a fool out of him, I could only
murmur that the Creator had beat us to it.

—Iilka Chase

Day Two, my brother came to the preliminary hearing on discovery, or something... I wasn't paying any attention to legal nuance; I was watching for legal treachery.

The prosecutor asked Randy, whose occupation was listed as 49ers professional football player, why he was missing practice.

Randy replied, "I came in here to tell you my brother Jerry didn't need 300 bucks. I owe him more that he could have any day."

"How much do you owe him?" the prosecutor questioned.

"Thousands," Randy said.

"If it's not going to impede a *pending* business deal or another good reason... could you tell the court *why*?"

Randy leaned in at him and said, "He negotiated my contract and we agreed he got 10% and the contract he got me was for $130,000... so 10% is thirteen thousand bucks."

"You ever give it to him?" the prosecutor queried.

"No."

"Why not?" the prosecutor asked, acting very perplexed.

"He wouldn't take it," Randy stated.

"Why not? Why wouldn't he take big money like that?" the prosecutor said, turning to the judge.

"He wouldn't take it," Randy said.

"Enlighten us further why he wouldn't take *thirteen* thousand dollars?"

"He's my brother."

Stunned by the reply, the prosecutor walked a tight circle before throwing his arm in the air and asked, "Exactly—and you're *under* oath—how did your brother come to earn this money?"

"He negotiated my football contract," Randy said, and he was tired of this bullshit... I knew my brother well... this prosecutor could be a Supreme Court judge, or the Pope... the fuse was lit. "Can I explain it to you real simple, Your Honor, and get outta here?"

"Go ahead," the judge said.

"They came to my mom and dad and offered me a $15,000 signing bonus and $15,000 for a season. My parents wanted me to take the contract. My brother said *no* and he was taking over. In two days he had an offer from the Lions for twice that much! We know Hollywood agents get 10% so we agreed he would get ten percent like they do."

"So your brother became your Hollywood agent?" the prosecutor interrupted, grasping at straws.

I knew something was coming and sure enough, Randy's voice went up an octave and he was ready to punch the prosecutor out.

"Yeah," Randy said. "He took me from an 8th round draft pick for 30 thousand dollars to the *fourth* pick of the draft with 130,000 dollars... I call that pretty *damn* good Hollywood negotiating, wouldn't you?"

The judge intervened, "Where are we going here... he said he owed his brother and now he told you why he owed him the money. He told you he would give him money at any time against their agreement."

"No further questions, Your Honor."

There was a little folderol from the Skunk and the Drunk before the judge stated, "We will reconvene early tomorrow. Unlike this one, I start a very complicated case tomorrow afternoon."

Chapter Thirty-Six

In ancient times they had no statistics,
so they had to fall back on lies.

—Stephan Leacock

A glass door with a small slot to receive a food tray through was the cell created to torture Federal prisoners in the Marin County Jail. I endured three days in one, somewhere in the same building the courtroom was. I lay next to that small slot sucking extra air for much of my three days in the glass box. Day Three of my trial offered a chance I could leave:

"Judge wants you to take the stand."

We agreed.

"And he's going to ask you where you got the phony bills. Say you don't know. You got them in one of many of your business transactions. Got that?" my lawyers said emphatically.

"I got it, and I better pee first," I agreed, exiting.

The Bow-Tie followed me into the bathroom. He wasted no time stating, "The judge is going to ask you one important question... Where'd you get the money? I understand it was from a sleazy informant or snitch."

"Right!" I answered, washing my hands.

"You say his name," Bow-Tie said, "Because if he is *any* value to them, which he must be, working for George Hunter White... they will not want another word about him in the public record. Ok. Tell your lawyers that old guy *really* stunk up the toilet."

The judge asked me and I said, "Sheldon Wolfe." My lawyers rose to their feet instantly, requesting a meeting in chambers.

"Denied. Any further questions for the defendant?" None and none. "We'll take a fifteen break and wrap up."

My lawyers began berating me... They *told* me not to say a name... "I just blurted out the truth. I'm sorry, but it didn't go *nowhere* did it?" I shrugged.

Acting exasperated, the Skunk and the Drunk went into conference with the prosecutor to "save me." I went to the toilet.

Bow-Tie whispered, "Now they are gonna work up a mistrial so both sides get their p's and q's fixed. They'll offer a mistrial. Do not take it. Demand judgment today."

I nodded in agreement.

Five minutes later, the prosecutor stood up and offered a mistrial. My lawyers had their response read back for accuracy by the court stenographer. "Against the advice of his attorneys, me, myself had refused... this that and the other."

Very soon and in legal terms the judge listed the bullshit. "Arresting agent said he was a felon and he had no record. And I certainly believe his brother when he said a few hundred dollars was immediately available to him, due to an honorable familial debt for what seemed to be $13,000-plus dollars the brother was emphatic that the defendant obtained for him."

The judge added a couple other points and told me: "You're free."

The telling thing as I left the courtroom was hearing the prosecutor's angry voice say to my lawyers, "You couldn't control your client and now I got a loss on my record."

Bow-Tie and I rode the same elevator down and out of the home of the suffocating glass cages and the Hall of Justice alone. Bow-Tie said, "They have a 97% conviction rate in that Federal court. So you're in the 3 percent."

Chapter Thirty-Seven

The advantage to telling the truth is nobody ever believes it.

—Dorothy Sayers

David Crosby, Mike Bloomfield and Jerry Garcia were born under the astrological sign of Leo. All three were gifted artists and performers.

Garcia's go-along, get-along demeanor is well documented. Bloomfield sadly was living his dream of being a blues musician. Unfortunately Bloomfield, born a millionaire, believed the Blues could only come from a place of rough despair, alcohol, drugs, cigarettes, and depression. From this life situation burst forth the good feeling of hope, happiness and a suggestion of romance.

Bloomfield of course had to self-create his own life into one of a "player that gets his guitar back from the loan shark the day of the gig!"

I saw a couple incredible rehearsals with him and the Paul Butterfield Blues Band at the heliport in Sausalito. Bloomfield was innovative,

focused and tossing out some funny lines to his bandmates.

At home he was despondent, sullen, chain-smoking and nipping at what was available.

David Crosby had the bad boy respect. He had done a month in jail for burglary, plus he was more than comfortable with knives, guns, and motorcycles and was very familiar with the seamy side of Hollywood.

Crosby came to his casual use of weapons and Harleys because his father was the cinematographer for 10 years on the Roger Corman "B" movies of which many had rough-and-tumble biker action. Like any kid would, Crosby hung out with the stuntmen. Stuntmen on films of the Corman genre would eager to share what real bikers, not actors, were like.

Crosby had ridden a bike up from LA when I met him. I, who had burned at top speed on bikes myself, helmetless, wearing cutoff Levis and flip-flops, gave Crosby's journey great respect.

He needed cannabis of course and was a true "aficionado" of the sinsemilla. Three tokes and he asked for my phone number.

Crosby had attended a French immersion school, knew how to sail, and could wax sentimental about and enjoy French wine. From his school days in Hollywood and the "stars" of the B movies who eventually emerged into being actual movie stars, Crosby had crossed artistic paths with many artists living in Laurel Canyon, LA.

On my Leo birthday, Sharon Tate and her friends were murdered. This is Crosby's version of what *really went down* just two or three weeks after the slaughter attributed to the Charles Manson family: Crosby's version of "what really happened— connect the loose dots and add a corrupt government with unlimited resources and immoral losers that'll do the dirtiest, sleaziest shit there could be."

"You ever cross paths with Manson or any of them?" Crosby asked.

"Luckily N.O.," I spelled out.

"Well," he replied... "First they manipulated him by taking him into some recording studio and recording songs. The girls he 'controlled'"—he emphasized the word with quote signs using his fingers—"believed there was a big recording deal and folk singing stardom just ahead. Don't matter to any degree 'cause they all livin' on starvation rations and LSD... *Always* plenty of that around in remote desert shacks where they used to make movies 20 years ago. They were just warm bodies stashed if needed for drug or anti-war bullshit... Maybe they say some Black Panthers kill 'em all. Then they can use that to shoot up some *Panthers* somewhere! That's what's goin' on... it's that deep."

Crosby said, "This is important. They take Tex, the killer that night, with Manson up to the house Terry Melcher and his fiancée Candice Bergan live in. Melcher was the Byrds' 'producer' because the record company forced them to have a 'producer' on their second album. We chose Melcher, a guy I went to school with, who would be happy to toke, hang out and stay out of the way."

It was a big nothing but it put Manson at the scene previously at the site of the murders. Melcher and Bergan move out, Polanski and Sharon Tate move in.

"Now we get to the Hollywood soap opera that in one form or another been goin' on around here since Hollywood was... So Sharon Tate had an actor she liked named Christopher Jones. More than liked... she liked sex with him.

"She marries Polanski, not exactly Mr. Suave, but Mr. Movie Director; old Hollywood story. She gets knocked up by Jones and so there are some confessions, truth, soap opera shit eventually... She's a *kid* from Texas.

"Here we speculate," Crosby digs in like a TV detective. "Who knows? Well, let's look at who was killed. One, the husband's oldest friend from way over in the tough streets of Poland. In a bitter moment you share with him the reality of the pregnancy. Two, his girlfriend Abigail Folger. One, there was a chance of 'pillow talk' between the two, and Folger, heir to the coffee fortune, was giving *big* bucks to radical black causes 'miminamim,'" Crosby emphasized. "You're gonna be compromised for that high society no-no."

"You're onto something," I injected.

Crosby turned his palms up and said, "Obvious stuff... Jones and Polanski are both in Europe working on the night of evil. Now look at the next victim, Jay Sebring, Sharon Tate's... *hairdresser*! Like they say, 'only your hairdresser *knows*.'" Crosby added, "The kid that got killed in the driveway was just wrong-place-wrong-time. Shot him and set off the bloodlust. And as I said earlier, Tex was the guy that brought Manson up there for the hokey music star tube meeting BS."

"It's got a ring of truth to it," I somewhat agreed.

"We'll see by how they play it in court with the sentencing," Crosby shrugged. "How they lay it out in court... See if Tex gets off easy 'cause he was working for the Man."

I said, "Í listen to those Paul Harvey radio vignettes faithfully. You know how Paul Harvey says, 'And that's the rest of the story'... I love that backstory... tidbits."

"Well here's something *new* for you," Crosby said, once again emphasizing the word with moving fingers. "Since *they* pulled the violent crap off, they do it again, somewhere, sometime."

Chapter Thirty-Eight

It is easier to get forgiveness than it is to get permission.

—Stewart's Law of Retroaction

Sam Cutler, the Rolling Stones' road manager, was the last person to jump in the band's helicopter to escape the violence surrounding the front and sides of the stage at the Altamont Festival. Cutler opened the door at Jerry Garcia and Mountain Girl's home on Madrone Street in Larkspur. I didn't know him but the English accent made me think he must have had something to do with the festival.

Sam Cutler, the Rolling Stones' road manager, in a backstage melee with fans, photographers and Hell's Angels in England.

"I'm Jerry and was supposed to come over today," I waved as I walked in.

The Stout sisters appeared, dressed in "total tie-dye" clothes for a month-long housekeeping job. It had to be something like that or Mountain Girl would not have them roaming her home, I thought. I had a warm verbal exchange with the well-known Deadheads, famous for their mantra, "We're here for the music, not the men or drugs... We've got our own." Interesting to me, with a little knowledge here and there of the three women, one was said to be able to drive 65, put her make-up on using the rearview mirror, and never miss a hit on that constant joint being passed around on the way to out-of-town shows.

"Come on in and sit down... you want a beer or something?... Sam Cutler," he said as we shook hands.

"Jerry told me to swing by couple days after the show," I offered. I threw out, "Brought a Ten Bob Dill, eh mate," in an attempt at an English accent. Ten Bob was slang for a specific amount of money, and Dill was short for Picadilly Circus, where the discreet cannabis dealers worked in whispers.

Cutler was in no mood for swapping insider cross-cultural references. "The family took off. I'm lookin' after the place for a couple more days," he said. "Needed a break after that disaster."

"Somebody got murdered fighting a Hell's Angel was the TV report. I had tickets for the Stones in LA, so I didn't go."

"I was the Stones' road manager. It was bloody ugly as any hooligan football brainbeater... The Stones fired me. The Garcias are givin' me a real break while it sorts out."

"Heat of the moment... They know how to reach

you?... How long you with 'em?" I suggested and questioned.

"They told me to stay with the equipment but I jumped on the chopper instead."

"Details are sketchy to me, Sam, because the people I know who went were all so far back they could only see some general mayhem in front of the stage, but not who or what or why," I stated.

"I bailed to save my life, man," Cutler said. Everything he said thereafter was expletive-loaded. "So Keith sez to me go see Don James and find out what the f— is goin' on. I go find him on stage. He's standin' on the back corner smiling, watching some Angels bust up some people... who are just getting pushed from behind *into* the Angels and their bikes! What's goin' on, I said to Don F—'ing James, and he says these Angels will kill somebody that touches their motorcycles. It's nuts.

Why, I jumped in that whirlybird, and I could have fallen out. Was Don 'All Knowing' James told me to look out in the crowd, scan here and there, and see the yellow pails... Then he pointed me toward one and over there and then... way to the back I see a yellow pail and I say I see the f—'ing people with yellow pails... So f—'ing what?"

I leaned in, exuding curiosity.

"So Don James says to me, 'They're passing out the psycho acid.'"

"Who's that's weirdo?" I asked Cutler. "Don James?"

"Don James is the guy the Americans give British groups... the biggest ones... a guarantee of no

147

drug busts during the tour, period."

"I could see a guy like that evolving. So many British groups end up leaving everything they make to lawyers 'cause of a pot arrest," I said matter-of-factly, pondering the thought.

"'Makes ya psychotic... this LSD... the type to give you a psychotic interlude. In an hour or so this place could blow up in madness if the stuff works,'" Sam said James told him.

"There was a wacko subplot going on?" I asked, amazed.

"Could have been Armageddon out there in those barren hills," Cutler said, like he was pleading for his job back... "Lotta Angels on the psycho acid... So I jumped in that helicopter!"

The Stout sisters appeared and one of them said, "Sam, that's Jerry B there? He's known to have greeeaaat weed."

"Plus... Lory, the world's greatest pie maker, is on her way with one," the older sister said, adding, "So munchie attack, we are ready."

"You're on," I said to the sisters, and to Sam I added, "Knowin' it like *you* did I wouldn't have been the *last* man in that chopper."

Next page, the Stout Sisters, left front row. L-R Susan Stout, Lory Barrish, Kathy Stout. From Rolling Stone Magazine, *Issue 66, "Evening With The Grateful Dead."*

Chapter Thirty-Nine

The worst thing about some men is when
they are not drunk, they are sober.

—William Butler Yeats

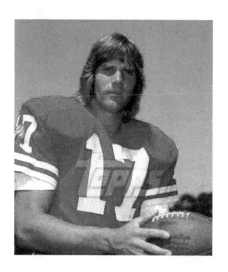 The gods of meeting erudite and lovely ladies in San Francisco's high-end Union Street singles scene blessed me with Adonis for a sidekick. John Isenbarger joined the 49ers fresh out of Indiana University. Six foot four with flowing golden locks, Ike, as he was nicknamed, had been surrounded by girls for so long he was relaxed about it all, making him easy and fun to be around.

The IU connection and his being a teammate of my brother gave us an initial bond. We soon were enjoying forays to not only Union Street but also the Trident. Ike blended in casually with the much more unusual mix of people in the Trident scene as well.

Football-wise, IU had been pathetic for decades, but the Golden One was instrumental in leading the Hoosiers to the Rose Bowl game, where they lost to

ST TEAM ALL-AMERICAN, 1967 & 196

the OJ Simpson-led USC Trojans. Ike was chosen to appear on the Late Night Johnny Carson TV show to hype the big game. Ike excelled on the football field, from the first practice for the 49ers to big games.

One evening on the way out of the Trident, we encountered three Hells Angels being grabby and giving unwanted attention to the hostess. Ike, not knowing the hippie delusion that Angels were swell guys, called them out. That sense of chivalry came out as a warning: "Leave her alone... She asked you *at least* twice!"

Instantly three Angels came forward and one pushed him. Ike pushed him back so strongly the other Angels broke his fall to the floor.

The action escalated quickly in both movement and noise and I had to jump in, grabbing and yelling. Busboys, bartenders, and men at the restaurant's entrance broke it up, but not before Ike landed a punch through the crowd.

Since the skirmish happened at the Trident, a regular source of colorful media news, the *San Francisco Chronicle* ran an article on two 49ers versus Hells Angels over some women. Cooler than cool was being mistaken for a 49er. It validated all the sit-ups, pushups and bodysurfing in the cold Pacific Ocean I did to stay in condition.

In the moment, however, Ike and I had

adrenaline poppin' so it was fortunate the night was still young.

Chapter Forty

Forgive your enemies, but remember their names.

—President John F. Kennedy

A wild, windswept rocky corner of Marin County named Bolinas was founded by Australian whale men. They used the large lagoon fed by the Pacific Ocean to shelter their boats.

Like the kids in Miller Beach, Indiana, there was hearty, ruddy, nature-driven looks. The touch of daredevil, entrepreneurial scallywag and swagger from the boys, some earthy and free-spirited independence from the girls. A pool hall bar open early, grocery store and café with outdoor seating.

It was a bit incongruous to see a suit and bow-tie seated alone at the café. I was carrying a bathing suit and towel on my way for a swim when I slipped uninvited into the seat across him. Bow-Tie glanced at the bathing suit and towel but said nothing.

"I saw you sitting here and just wanted to thank you. Actually beyond thank you, and no more."

"Tony said he'd checked you out and couldn't get a bad word. A true believer in going towards the light."

"That's the greatest possible thing I could hear to wrap up what I hope was *the* more horrid, terrible period of time in my life."

Bow-Tie looked at his watch and said, "Tony will be here in three minutes. Every one of those minutes is a precious one and I must be alone."

"I understand," I nodded, getting up.

"No," Bow-Tie asked, "Give me two of those three minutes."

"Sure," I answered, sitting down.

"Are you thinking of payback... tires slashed, or someone beat up?"

"Violent thoughts never occurred. No vengeance. None. When I was in college I took a course in Comparative Religions. There were from two or three to six, eight pages on Hindu, Islam, Zoroaster," I highlighted, "Buddhism. All of 'em. One thing I learned... It overlapped with my Methodist upbringing of: 'what goes around comes around.' The law of karma in Buddhism is the same thing, only more precious with deeper explanations. I've never seen it fail."

"Pay attention to who's around you," Bow-Tie said. "Until this Viet-Nam War is over, it's going to be open season on perceived traitors."

From where we were sitting to the end of Wharf Road, the lagoon exchanged water with the sea. About a hundred yards toward the open ocean, there was a perfect sun and only a breeze. With a, "It's been fantastic to run into you today..."

Bow-Tie nodded, "Yes."

... I was ready to grab that glorious moment nature was offering. "Please tell Serra I'm gonna play it dumb... like I never figured *anything* out. I'm going for a swim," I added with a smile.

"Aren't you afraid of a shark attack?" Bow-Tie questioned.

"You and I have interacted... exchanged, if you will, and I think you would agree; people should fear the land sharks more."

Big Red Ted's Confession

Red Ted wearing the Cohasset Cannabis commemorative t-shirt, Kathmandu 1974.
Photo: Bill Wassman

Big Red Ted was on a gurney in what was proclaimed as the number one cancer fighting hospital in the U.S.A. Then Uncle Sam pulled the money plug.

It was a three-day overland journey to Minneapolis and the Mayo Brothers Clinic. It made Big Red Ted angry because in many ways he did deep dirty deeds for Uncle Sam, but wasn't *official*, so no benefits. Big Red Ted was "flipped" to get the job.

Here's how it went down. On his way home from the Peace Corps he had mailed fifty grams of Kashmiri hashish to his lady love, waiting for him in Indiana. Her kid brother finds it... tells the parents... they tell the police. They're waiting for Ted, so he and she are busted. *Serious crime* is smuggling hash into the USA. Since her parents turned her in, Ted's lady love got a harsh, supervised five years' probation and her night in jail. They offered Big Red Ted a year less a day, counting his one night in jail, because he was coming from the two years in the Indian desert. It was to be served in a Club Fed. It was a sentencing break the Peace Corps initiated. *Or* Big Red Ted could become a rat?

He had spent two nights on my couch and the second day was People's Park, and he left to get his hash and girlfriend. My brother's name only came up as, "He's playing with the 'Niners and they're getting good."

"I can get you a National Football League player that deals weed," Big Red Ted told his new handlers. The government, television and print news would love a big splash like that. Big Red Ted gets a sixty-day stay of his sentencing to produce a felony arrest. Big Red Ted headed to California to set up my brother Randy, his college teammate, through me.

Much to his dismay, I would reveal in a casual conversation that my brother was married with a second child due any day. Pot use nil, drinking less than daily! He was a serious pro player with a new three-year contract.

Big Red Ted begins his confession by listing all the things he did for me to make up for getting *me* arrested—his friend on whose couch he had spent many a night watching my scene come and go. But that sixty-day clock was expiring.

Plus, when he started working on me he discovered The Squirrel, who provided anti-war eyes and ears in the Bay Area. The Squirrel had crossed paths with Ted five years before as a "football player chaser," with the players-initiated nickname Big Red remembered from many years before. Any cannabis bust filled Ted's felony requirement. In California it was a one-to-ten felony for a seed or roach.

Ted: "The Squirrel insisted there's bags of money someplace, somewhere. One of them has the ear of George Hunter White and *he* takes over. The rest is history."

"Three days in the glass tomb, three days in the courthouse and walking out with the three percent," I spit at him over the phone.

As I stated and shall list, Big Red Ted did many things to pay me back over forty years. It's ironic however that my brother would repeat, "I don't know how you stay friends with that guy... He's a coward and you *never* associated yourself with a coward." I'd answer my brother with much of Ted's payback list: the genesis for my very successful Tibetan carpet business. Also Ted arranged the greatest Himalayan trek for me that allowed me to be the second Westerner to visit the Ganeesh Himal; only Jess, a French mapmaker, had been there before in 1955. Ted got Jess' maps, which were integral to a spectacular adventure. In addition, I enjoyed being at the American Embassy when a slideshow of the trek was used to open for the movie "The American Assault on Everest."

Big Red Ted introduced me to Tom and Margo Pritzker, owners of Hyatt Hotels. There was a shared love of horseback riding and side forays to the

Schubert Theatre to see *Cats*. They had "behind the dugout" seats for the White Sox. We all attended the twenty-fifth anniversary show of The Grateful Dead at the Shoreline venue, a nice cross-country friendship for a couple of years with the Pritzkers. They attended the minor Royal Wedding as well as Ted and I.

Big Red had footed the bill for a fifty-person New York City 40th birthday party for me; Ted was in the Big Apple for allegedly a major Tibetan artifact sale when he knew I was in the city with CSN.

All these and more I'd tell Randy. He would always get the last word: "If push comes to shove in one of these exotic places you see him in, remember... Coward."

Red Ted was assigned to Mylan Melvin. Melvin was an anti-war snitch at the University of California Berkeley campus. He came out with a blubbering admission on the number one listened-to rock radio station. Hippies were delusional and believed him. His assignment was to bust Joan Baez's husband David Harris, a very high-profile, buttoned-down scholarly type, an image that made him a major threat.

As intelligent, worldly and sincere as the Baez sisters were, Mylan Melvin cracked them. Here's how: he went from openly admitted anti-war snitch to suddenly having a budget for camera crew, engineers and experienced Hollywood heavyweights for a "no experience whatsoever" Melvin production, the *Big Sur Festival*. Mimi Fariña, Joan Baez's younger sister and musical attraction in her own right, was the headliner. Crosby, Stills, Nash and Young agreed to one song. Big Red Ted worked as Melvin's gopher. His wife was rewarded with a perfectly lighted crowd reaction shot.

The big Hollywood production made it heady stuff. Fariña would take the perfect see-God, make-you-fall-in-love psychedelic. She would rush into a marriage with Melvin. It lasted two weeks, Fariña told me years later, though it took nearly a year to finalize the divorce due to Melvin's obstruction, so he could continue to pretend it was a happy marriage.

Melvin got his man. David Harris went to jail.

Melvin wrote a memoir aptly titled, *The High Life of a Lowlife*.

Joan Baez with her husband, activist and Stanford student body president David Harris, in 1968. Later that year, Harris would be convicted of refusing induction into the Army. Mylan Melvin shadowing, left.

Next, Big Red Ted confessed to his unique role in the "Dope Raid on a Lawyer's House," as the *San Francisco Chronicle* headlined. All the cannabis lawyers were under one roof to celebrate a new legal partnership and office: Patrick Hallinan, Tony Serra and Michael Stepanian, famous for being The Grateful Dead's lawyer and writing a column in *High Times* magazine on the ins and outs of cannabis arrests... and how to beat them. The raid had 23 narcotics officers, including the heads of both the Sacramento and Los Angeles jurisdictions. As they assembled, the *Chronicle* would document, an argument began between a prosecutor and Patrick Hallinan. Hallinan knocked him out. From the *Chronicle*, "it was a perfect left hook." The lawyers and their wives, tsk tsk, were a quick exit. Myself, encouraged to attend by Big Red Ted, and having enjoyed interacting with Stepanian as I had hoped, left as well.

With a search warrant based on an informant who "smelled marijuana, the agents... entered and arrested fifty-seven people." To give the host lawyer cover, he was to be arrested with the other "long gone" lawyers. Ted was to be arrested with him and protect him from harm during the night in jail. It happened.

It was big enough nationally that *Rolling Stone* magazine did a two-part, in-depth article on the attempt to waylay pro-cannabis lawyers. Big Red Ted is quoted in *Rolling Stone* on details of how the raid was conducted. Before his confession I always assumed he was quoted because he *had* been arrested. Like the shyster, it gave him cover, too.

I would use his *Rolling Stone* quote as an example of what the Freedom of Information Act had clarified: the actions and role of the people he was "outing."

"They can black out 90% of the names but eventually you can connect the dots. I read mine," and thus told Big Red he was confirming what I knew or suspected.

Big Red Ted must have been close enough to some kind of "informant action" throughout his life or he would not have thought the agency would pop for his medical bills. I assume it was something to do with or about the Tibetan exile community. He lived in Kathmandu from college until his final year.

His list of paybacks to me for his harmful betrayal would have me counter with, "When you were in on the hokey fake bills crap, I lost a lady that had the other round-the-world plane ticket with me. *Must* have been something special. She wanted three kids with me."

Big Red Ted confessed, "I got her number out of your phone book while you were in the shower. The Squirrel called her, saying you gave her the number to say bon voyage. The Squirrel called back in half an hour and warned her that your lawyer had called and said Jerry was arrested and she better get out of town. Potential witness or testimony gone clean," Red Ted said matter-of-factly... adding, "There was heavy planning to your arrest, because you were supposed to have $50k." Big Red knowing that number was a dot connector... I had never revealed it.

He would point out that he rented me a town car

so I could not only attend but arrive in "proper fashion" to the Lord David Forbes' Royal Wedding.

"Three days in a glass tomb," I would reply rhetorically, "Versus a social highlight?"

Time tempered by his passing and his confession... I forgave him. He introduced me to the Dalai Lama, which led to me meeting the Dalai Lama two years later alone, when His Holiness

Red Ted at the wedding of Lord David Forbes.
Photo: Tom Pritzker

would direct me to the Hemis Festival in Ladakh. This journey takes one to where space begins, time

is fluid, all centered in a civilization that has existed without war for 2500 years. As I later covered the Dalai Lama's arrival in Hawaii as a journalist for two newspapers, His Holiness recognized me and came through a throng of media, and I was able to tell him I had gone to Ladakh and how meaningful it was. His Holiness was happy.

I forgave Big Red and put him in *The Bandit of Kabul* with none of his confession. The main reason being many of these sleazoids are still around with reputations to protect. Plus the more I played it dumb the more I found out.

"Hey," Red Ted said from the waiting room in the Mayo Clinic. "It could have been a lot worse than that for you. When I was looking for help behind that prison time I was facing for that hash bust, I was contacted by an old fraternity brother, Thomas Charles Huston, who I'm sure you know now was in the top echelon of the White House."

"The infamous Thomas Charles Huston, who planned with Nixon?" I asked.

"That's the guy, yeah, and he hated your guts. He said so when I started talking about a way to avoid jail time."

"Why did he hate me... I never met him at IU."

"You pulled the plug on Bo Diddley at our big spring frat party. Remember that?"

"I pulled the plug because the fake waterfall was broken, and the band was playing electric while standing in a pool of water! What kind of idiot would hate me for that?"

"Well, the Police Record shows that ole Tom Huston had a pretty twisted mind. Maybe he wanted to see Bo Diddley fry... just being sarcastic... the nurse is calling me."

He hung up the phone.

164

Chapter Notes

The body at best
Is a bundle of ashes
Longing for rest
It cries when it wakes

—Edna St. Vincent Millay

Chapter One
Betty Larsen is the girl
mentioned in the open-
ing Chuck Berry quote.

Chapter Two
An article fragment
about one of my life-
guard rescues.

Breaks Ne
In Shallov
Water Div

A 21-year-old Rockfor
man suffered a broken
in a shallow dive at
Street beach yesterday
ing.

John Schliecher took
six running steps or
beach and dived into a
bar, according to Jerry
ler, 17, of 7040 Locus
the lifeguard who re
Schliecher.

Schliecher was tak
Mercy Hospital.

Kampus Korner

"Welcome home", we repeat, to our Miller college students, who are home for the summer vacation period. It's good to see all of them again.

Jerry Beisler, son of Mr. and Mrs. Ed Beisler of 7940 Locust, is working as a lifeguard at Marquette Park Beach this summer. Jerry will return for his sophomore year at I. U. this Fall..

Chapter Three
Roy Pratt taught in the Gary, Indiana school system, and after he retired was elected Councilman from his district. He is credited with creating the Minor League baseball park and Casino, among his other accomplishments.

An article from my IU days.

Chapter Four
Larry Lindeen was a high school friend attending Mexico City College. He became my dorm roommate at the school and remains a friend for life. We enjoyed the Norteño music and food vendors found in many a weekend plaza fiesta, and he attended my Cinco de Mayo game. Myself, Doreen, Lindeen and his date were escorted out of a bullfight for cheering for the bull. Larry became an attorney.

Chapter Eleven
My roommate Frank Brennan became the Stanford University women's tennis coach, his teams winning the NCAA tournament 6 times.

Also in 1969 and relevant to this book: Booker T proved he had learned well at Indiana University when he turned down the offer to provide the song for a Hollywood movie starring James Coburn. Coburn was a "hot box office" attraction but

Hollywood wanted the publishing rights to "Time is Tight."
Booker T turned Hollywood down, and the song was quickly
signed to a solid contract to be the theme song for another film,
"Uptight."

*Chapter
Seventeen*
Paul Bucha's
Congressional
Medal of Honor
award was by
far the biggest
achievement
in an extended
family of over-
achievers.

ART GREENSPON / *Associated Press* 1968

Chapter Nineteen
Randy Beisler played 11 years in the NFL for Philadelphia,
San Francisco and Kansas City. He started 49 games and
participated in 5 playoff games with San Francisco. He was
recently voted into the Indiana Football Hall of Fame.

Two party participants, Jackie Horvath (left) and Carol (right).

Chapter Twenty
In the Bahamas with Sally Pierce.

Chapter Twenty-Four
"Susie Q" and "Little Latin Lupe Lu" were hit songs.

Chapter Twenty-Six
Yoshiko married a Danish underground filmmaker and moved to Denmark.

Chapter Twenty-Eight
Photographer and documentarian Sam D'Alisio chronicled Mayan civilization and the pre-cartel Mexican cannabis

era, including a relocated Lebanese clan that made hashish for the Amsterdam market in a remote mountain village. He also captured the action around the clandestine airstrips.

Chapter Twenty-Nine
People's Park still exists and hosts events commemorating the battle and march. The University of California still claims the land.

Chapter Thirty-Three
When George Hunter White died, his wife left his diary to Foothill College, where I read it. After government agents came in and flagrantly removed some pages, the school transferred the diary to the Bing Library at Stanford University for greater protection.

Chapter Thirty-Seven
On August 8, the day of the Sharon Tate murders, the Beatles were photographed crossing Abbey Road for the iconic album photo. Tex Watson, as David Crosby predicted, would serve his time in a minimum security prison near his hometown and father four children while incarcerated there. The Manson girls are dying in prison.

Jan. 15: San Francisco Superior Court Judge Francis McCarty urged state legislators to reduce "horrendous mandatory State prison sentences" for marijuana and narcotic users. In a letter to State Senator George Moscone he said the law "betrays a degree of hysteria" in dealing so harshly with the "user trapped in his addiction." The "fury" of the law should fall not on the victims but on the "profit-making dealers" in drugs. Presently, he said, "a second conviction of possessing even a fifth of a marijuana cigarette calls for a mandatory two-year

State prison sentence." A second conviction for possession of a narcotic results in imprisonment for not less than five years with no hope of parole.

Chapter Twenty-Five
From a retrospective in the *San Francisco Chronicle,* an excerpt concerning drug laws in 1969.

Chapter Thirty-One
Photo from my entrance/ exit visa to the Atlas Mountains area of Morocco.

Chapter Thirty-Three
The Grateful Dead were crusaders early in the collective career, as witnessed by the benefit to end prohibition they played under the threat of mass arrest. On May 29, 1966, police ringed the venue.

Chapter Thirty-Eight

Don James appears in two Rolling Stones documentaries. In one, James assists Stones guitarist Keith Richards in throwing a television out of a 10-story window into a parking lot below. James can also be seen in onstage photos of the Allman Brothers Band. The only reference to James in print is by *San Francisco Chronicle* writer Joel Selvin, who claims James was in the Witness Protection Program.

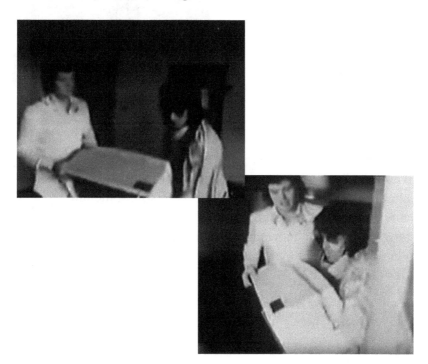

Chapter Thirty-Nine

In 1974, the World Football League was formed to challenge the now merged NFL-AFL. The WFL offered to double a player's current salary as a signing bonus, plus again double their salary for a one-season contracst. John Isenbarger signed and played for the Hawaiian team, earning in one year what he had in two previous seasons with the 49ers.

Though the WFL drew 80,000 fans to its championship game, the League folded after that initial season.

Chapter Forty
Tony Serra's most infamous
legal case was made into a
movie starring James Woods
and Robert Downey, Jr. The
government had convicted
Serra's Korean-American
client of murder to keep the
actual two-time murderer
available as an informant. The
government implored Serra
not to free the innocent man,
for the "greater good" in the
Drug War.

Big Red Ted's Confession
Thomas Charles Huston is notorious for the plan named
after him. Offered to and accepted by Nixon, it included
concentration camps in Mexico for anti-war resisters. All his
other insidious schemes were to be implemented in Huston
Plan B, which removed the camps but kept the sleazy plots
from Plan A.

About the Author

 Jerry Beisler is the author of *The Bandit of Kabul,* chronicling the decade of 1970-1980, and *The Berkeley Years,* a hardback coffee table compilation of magazine articles, newspaper features, reviews, political commentary, a novella, and new poetry. Beisler's previous books of poetry are *Mother Asia and Cousin California* and *St. Elvis and Missionary Thought* (Print Mint Press Publishing), and *Hawaiian Life and The Pink Dolphins* (Raindance Publishing).

Beisler attended Indiana University, Mexico City College, and San Francisco State University. He has lived for extended periods of time in some of the planet's most remote corners.

Additional work available at:
payhip.com/b/svg9
payhip.com/b/xm4p

About the Cover Artist

Andrew Annenberg's path was set at age 7 when he declared, "I would like to be an artist when I grow up." His artistic forays led him to oil painting at age 14, to which he has been devoted ever since. Visionary and surreal elements weave throughout all Annenberg's work. He lived for thirty years in Maui, where he held numerous one-man and group shows. His time in Hawaii inspired him to focus on marine environments, particularly dolphins. Recently, he has been inspired by the beauty of Northern California with an emphasis on the giant oak trees with water, as well as experimenting with chalk pastels. He and Jerry Beisler have been collaborators for over 40 years. "This latest was very fun and made me laugh as I painted it."

For inquiries, visit:
AAmasterworks.com

CPSIA information can be obtained
at www.ICGtesting.com
Printed in the USA
FSHW020743240420
69339FS